TRADITIONAL
INDONESIAN
TEXTILES

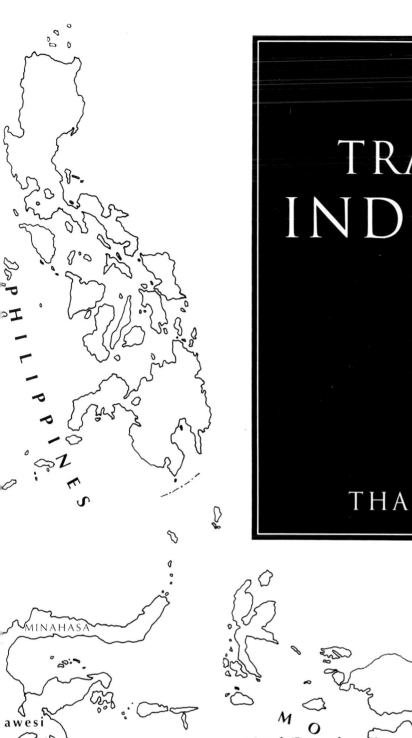

JOHN GILLOW

TRADITIONAL INDONESIAN TEXTILES

PHOTOGRAPHS BY
BARRY DAWSON

237 Illustrations, 188 in colour

THAMES AND HUDSON

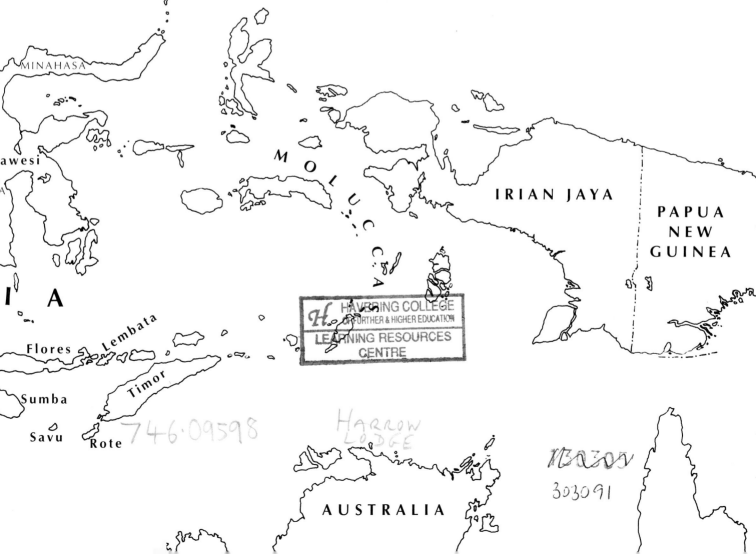

PHILIPPINES

MINAHASA

awesi

A

M O L U C C A S

IRIAN JAYA

PAPUA
NEW
GUINEA

I A

Flores

Lembata

Sumba

Timor

Savu

Rote

HARROW
LODGE

AUSTRALIA

For Luke, Nicola, Jenny, Joel, Seth and Joseph

Contents

Sido mukti, a batik motif much favoured in Surakarta, central Java.

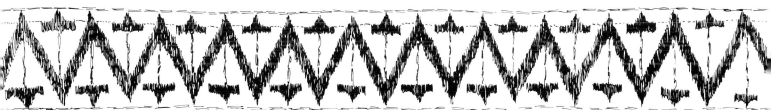

Preface

Throughout our travels in the outer islands of Indonesia we were met with unfailing courtesy, and at every weaving village we visited – once we had won the villagers' trust – they would offer to show us round. The scene that would greet us was one to be repeated wherever we stopped, in Sumba, Rote and Timor, in Sulawesi and Kalimantan: hanks of cotton warp threads, with minutely spaced ikat ties, dyed indigo-blue or *kombu* red, were hung about every house. Young girls were helping their mothers to lay out the ikat-patterned warp threads, while their grandmothers sat in the cool recess underneath the stilted houses, weaving narrow widths of cloth on the simplest of backstrap looms.

To leave the outer islands – the pageantry of the *pasola* mock-cavalry battle in Sumba, the all-consuming burial feasts of the Toraja, the shy splendour of the west Timorese villagers and the simple dignity of the Rotenese, and to return to the sophistication of Bali, Java and Sumatra, was not a matter for regret, however, but anticipation at the joys of further exploration. Bali, with its love of festivity and drama and its idiosyncratic, syncretic religion, has a wealth and range of textiles unrivalled in the Indonesian archipelago outside the large, rich island of Sumatra. And then to Java, crowded with people, *becak* drivers, market women selling fruit and vegetables and Chinese merchants in their shops, all either wearing, making, transporting or selling batik cloth. Everywhere the smell of batik wax permeated the air, from the shops outside the Pasar Klewer in Solo with their batik-making materials, to Cirebon, where by the Kanoman *kraton* the smell of wax intermingles with that of fried crab in ginger and soy sauce.

In all the islands that Barry and I visited, textiles are painstakingly crafted, either for domestic use, for everyday wear, for ritual purposes or, more commonly in the Indonesian heartland, for commercial sale. And it is with these textiles, excepting some from Sarawak in Malaysian Borneo which relate closely to those of Kalimantan, that this book concerns itself. I have sought to show the range of textiles that are still being produced in Indonesia today, from the sophisticated market-orientated fabrics created by the techniques of batik, plangi, tritik weft-ikat or *songket*, to the carefully crafted warp-ikat hand-weaving for the home or for sacred use, made by the women of the outlying societies. In all cases, however, the textiles of Indonesia are made in a manner sanctioned by tradition in a society where there is an almost organic relationship between the producer and consumer of textiles, and in which textiles play such a vital symbolic role that the production of anything resembling inferior craftsmanship would be seen as a blow against the very essence of the Indonesian identity.

Songket end panel of a *geringsing* double-ikat cloth made in Tenganan Pegeringsingan, Bali.

7

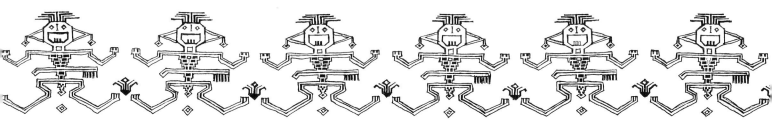

1   The Textile History of Indonesia

More than 13,000 islands make up the Indonesian archipelago, which stretches 3,500 miles from northern Sumatra to Irian Jaya, the Indonesian part of New Guinea. Indonesians call their country 'Tanah Air Kita', meaning 'our land-water', for much of Indonesian territory is in fact sea. The Indonesian peoples form part of the Austronesian language group whose members inhabit a vast area encompassing Indonesia, Malaysia, the Philippines, Taiwan, Micronesia, Melanesia, Polynesia, and even Madagascar, off the coast of Africa.

The population of Indonesia, as in most other Third World countries, has continued to expand rapidly in the years after World War II, so much so that it is now the world's fifth most populous state. Most of the islands, however, are uninhabited due to their size (many are little more than atolls) and the vast majority of people – about ninety per cent – live on the three major islands of Sumatra, Java and Bali. Java and Bali are very densely populated, Sumatra much less so. The rest of the islanders are sparsely spread through Kalimantan (Indonesian Borneo), Sulawesi (the erstwhile Celebes), the Nusa Tenggara chain that extends from tropical Bali eastwards to the dry, hot islands of Lombok, Sumbawa, Sumba, Savu, Rote, Flores and Timor, and the many smaller islands to the north and east. The archipelago is home to many different peoples of great cultural diversity, yet these peoples manage to retain an underlying unity that manifests itself in the ancient beliefs, customs and social organization of each cultural group.

The warm tropical climate of these equatorial islands varies little in temperature, and the monsoon winds bring a rainy season that in most of the archipelago lasts from November to April. It is a region of intense volcanic activity, and unsurprisingly these volcanic mountains hold great mystical significance for the people, who portray them in their textile art. The volcanoes of Java serve a most beneficial function, for they produce lava that is alkaline rather than acidic, forming soil that is extremely fertile – so fertile that it frequently yields three crops of rice a year. This agricultural wealth provided a base on which it was possible to construct the kind of sophisticated society equipped to create great religious and architectural masterpieces such as the giant stupa at Borobudur. In addition, not only could the rich courts of Java afford the time and costly materials needed to produce complex and beautiful textiles themselves, they also created a ready market for exotic foreign cloth. Whether from home or abroad, sophisticated textiles were worn not just for adornment but more importantly for prestige. The settled agriculture of Java, Bali and parts of Sumatra had little counterpart in the outlying islands where slash-and-burn agriculture was the norm, but even there local courts channelled their riches from the spice trade and other sources into the ostentatious display of home-woven and imported cloth.

Indonesia lies at the crossroads between the great civilizations of China to the north east and India, Arabia and Europe to the north west. Continual waves of foreign invaders, colonizers, missionaries, merchants and traders were to pass through the straits of the archipelago, bringing with them cultural changes that were to have a marked effect on the development of the textiles of the region. The depth of this cultural change was felt most deeply in what might be said to be the heartland of the Indonesian peoples, on the coast of Sumatra, throughout Java, Madura and Bali and on the Kalimantan and Sulawesi littorals. These were the richer lands which enjoyed

A border of Iban Dyak head-hunters wearing plumed swords worked in *sungkit*, from a *kalambi* jacket, Sarawak.

(Opposite) A *sirimpi* woman dancer from central Java wearing a *patola* waistcloth and a *plangi*-decorated waistsash.

9

An ancient bronze kettle drum (face, side view and motifs) from the Dong-Son region of northern Vietnam, collected in south-western China in the 1920s.

greater resources than the mountainous inland jungles or the outlying islands of the archipelago. The impact of this long contact with foreigners is shown in the sophistication of the textiles produced in these regions, the foremost example being Sumatra, with its extensive range of textile techniques. Techniques for weaving *songket* and weft ikat on discontinuously warped looms were introduced into the Indonesian heartland in this way, as were the resist-dyeing techniques of plangi and tritik.

Between the eighth and second century BC, because of military pressure from China, there was a large-scale migration from the Annam region of northern Vietnam, bringing to Indonesia a culture known to historians as the Dong-Son, which was to have a tremendous impact on the archipelago. It is widely believed that the backstrap continuously warped loom arrived with the Dong-Son, as did the art of warp-ikat. The Dong-Son were masters of bronzework and used bronze kettle drums in their rituals. On these drums were designs of the soul ship, the tree of life and the geometric patterns of the rhomb and key, spirals, sunbursts and human and animal forms that were to be diffused widely through the islands and to reappear as textile designs. Many of these are still in use in places as geographically separate as Sumatra and Timor. A fresh wave of migration from south China brought to Indonesia a culture known as the Late Chou, which introduced certain asymmetric designs and had particular influence in Borneo. The Bataks of north Sumatra, the Toraja of central Sulawesi, the Dyaks of Borneo and the islanders of east Nusa Tenggara and the southern Moluccas were to be largely unaffected by later foreign cultural influences, however, but continued to weave warp-ikat textiles out of rough homegrown cotton with Dong-Son-inspired designs, dyed with locally gathered dyestuffs.

The most pervasive post-Dong-Son foreign influence was that of India. By the second century AD Indian traders had made contact with the coastal peoples of Java and by the fifth century a Hindu kingdom had been established in Java. In the seventh century the kingdom of Srivijaya was founded in south Sumatra (around modern Palembang), which was to become a major centre of Mahayana Buddhism. Its political influence was to be felt right up through the Malayan peninsula as far away as northern Thailand. Regional power passed in the mid-ninth century to the Javanese kingdom of Mataram, where an amalgam of Indian Buddhism, Hinduism and Javanese animism resulted in an architectural style that produced glorious temple structures. In the wake of the Mataram era a succession of Hindu kingdoms held sway over the archipelago, with their capitals situated in east or central Java. The last flowering of the Hindu-Buddhist era was the Javanese Majapahit Empire (1294–1478), which was to disintegrate under the impact of Islam. From India, too, came the Hindu epics of the *Ramayana* and the *Mahabharata*, the source of the mask and *wayang* puppet dramas of Java and Bali. *Wayang* motifs appear in *geringsing* double ikat, the weft ikat of Bali and the tourist batik of Java.

The coming of Islam to Java and Sumatra in the fifteenth century with Indian and Arab Muslim traders and missionaries sounded the death-knell of the Hindu-Buddhist era on the islands, leading to the fall of the Majapahit Empire and the flight of the Javanese aristocracy to the shelter of neighbouring Bali. The spread of Islam would seem to have had little direct effect on Indonesian textiles, with the exception of some batik prayer cloths made in Jambi and Palembang in Sumatra, and in north Java for the Sumatran market, which are embellished with quotations from the Koran in Arabic script. It also led to the heightening of decorative embellishment and the lessening of the figurative element in Javanese batik.

It was the Muslim merchants, however, that brought the all-pervasive check or plaid design used for sarongs, in which the Malay seafarers were soon clad. They also

Chiefs from Mandi Angin, Jambi.

The Sultan of Jogjakarta wearing a batik *kain* in the royal *parang rusak* design, and trousers of *patola* silk double ikat.

introduced to the islands the most influential textile of them all, the fabled double-ikat silk *patola* cloth of Gujarat and the surrounding areas of north-west India. *Patola* cloth is considered to have magical properties and is treated as a sacred heirloom in places as remote as Irian Jaya. Its motifs have been copied and incorporated into cloths that themselves had sacred connotations, by different peoples right the way across the archipelago. The eight-stemmed *patola* motif pattern (called *jelamprang* in Indonesia) was so revered that in 1769 the Sultan of Surakarta reserved it, along with other batik patterns, for his family's exclusive use. Throughout Indonesia, strict rules specified which textiles were to be worn at every level of society. The sultans of central Java would periodically lay down stringent penalties for transgressions of these sumptuary rules, and it is said that the kings of Sumba could enforce the Sumban dress code until the 1920s. Sumban society was strictly divided, and textiles of increasing complexity of weave, variety of colouring and size were accorded to each stratum. Slaves dressed in plain-coloured, rather small *kain* waistcloths, whereas kings would wear vast, many coloured, warp-ikatted *hinggi* mantles, adorned with the special symbols of power and mystical significance reserved for royalty.

One indication of the value of cloth in Indonesian societies is given by the crucial role it played in the spice trade that first brought European adventurers to the archipelago. The spice islanders of the Moluccas, the world's first source of cloves, were reluctant to take silver and gold (which, in any case, the Europeans only had in short supply) for their precious spices, but were eager to trade them for the painted, printed, brocaded or ikatted cotton and silk cloths brought in abundance from the Indian coast. The

A Chinese-derived stork motif executed in *cap* batik on a sarong from the north Java coast.

Portuguese first sailed to the Moluccas at the beginning of the sixteenth century, but by 1600 the Dutch had ousted both the Portuguese and the interloping merchants of the English East India Company from most of the archipelago. The Dutch founded their capital of Batavia on Java in 1618 and from then on directly dominated Java, Sumatra and, indirectly, the rest of the archipelago. Dutch colonization produced profound changes in certain areas, notably in the Minahasa peninsula of Sulawesi and the central Moluccas, where the peoples were converted to Christianity while their original culture was largely eradicated. Elsewhere amongst the outlying islands the Dutch stayed largely in the background, and throughout Indonesia conducted most of their business by way of Chinese middlemen. Indeed, the Dutch policy of indirect rule in the long run tended to preserve local textile and other crafts.

Chinese traders established themselves on the coasts of Sumatra, Kalimantan, and Sulawesi (to which they brought the techniques of sericulture in the seventeenth century). It was the Chinese funeral custom to bury all personal possessions with the dead, and thus whole areas became great treasure-troves of exquisite Ming porcelain. Porcelain and Chinese embroideries – also important trade goods – were used as textile design sources. The most significant Chinese-derived motif was the Feng-Huan, or phoenix bird (a Chinese sign of virtue and benevolence). The phoenix motif appears on Javanese silk and cotton batiks. The *banji*, or Chinese swastika emblem, was used as a border motif in Balinese and Sumatran weft-ikat and in Javanese and Sumatran batik. Most picturesque of all are the cloud designs so characteristic of Chinese painting, which are such a striking feature of the batiks of Cirebon on the north Java coast.

The Chinese were prominent in the development of the Javanese batik block-printing industry in the latter part of the nineteenth century. Their crucial entrepreneurial role, combined with their ceremonial requirements for cloth embellished with Chinese religious symbols, encouraged the dissemination of Chinese motifs throughout the batik produced on the north Java coast. This eclectic industry also derived inspiration from such diverse sources as the beautiful painted south-east Indian chintzes and (at a later date) Dutch Art-Deco designs, in vogue at the famous atelier of the Eurasian Mrs Eliza Van Zuylen.

The Dutch East India Company was to collapse at the end of the eighteenth century after a rash of adverse speculation on the Amsterdam stock exchange, and the Dutch government took over the administration of the Indonesian islands, thus beginning the Dutch colonial empire. In the nineteenth century the Dutch expanded their trade in foreign cloth and Javanese batik, and penetrated the whole archipelago with these goods. The increased volume of trade had a number of far-reaching consequences. In Java itself it resulted in the introduction of the *cap* block-printing process into the batik industry, quickening and increasing production, and in the initial expansion of cotton-growing in Java and local production of the finely woven cloth that batik requires. It later led, however, to the eclipse of the Javanese cotton industry, as the requirements of the batik industry could be more easily and more economically satisfied with cheap imports of cloth from Europe, Egypt, India and Japan.

In many of the outlying islands the cheap, readily available, imported foreign cloth and Javanese *cap*-printed batik quickly ousted locally woven cloth from everyday use. Consequently, in many areas weaving ceased and home-woven textiles were put away, acquiring the status of sacred heirlooms. Weaving by no means ceased in all the outlying societies, however. Among the Batak of north-central Sumatra, for instance, the efficacy of vital rituals is dependent on the weaving of fresh textiles specifically for them, as it is in the Nusa Tenggara chain of islands, where weaving is prolific.

The Dutch took direct control of the outlying islands at the beginning of the twentieth century. They annexed southern Bali in 1906, with the tragic slaughter outside the royal palaces of the whole of the Badung Court, clad in their ritual finery. In terms of textiles, Dutch influence was felt most directly in the north Java batik industry, and Dutch-inspired motifs, rampant lions copied from Dutch coins and rajas dressed in their official Dutch frock coats appeared in the warp-ikat *hinggi* mantles of Sumba.

Dutch rule was effectively brought to an end by the Japanese invasion of 1942. Though the Japanese were initially welcomed as liberators from white colonial domination, the end of their brief, harsh rule was met with widespread relief. The Japanese had two direct influences on textile production in Indonesia. One was the intensive cultivation of cotton on Timor in an attempt to satisfy the pressing demand for cloth from a Japan at war. The other was that, due to the lack of cloth of all kinds, particularly the fine imported cambric needed for *tulis* batik work, many *tulis* workers faced destitution through loss of employment. To combat this, workshops in Pekalongan, run by Eliza Van Zuylen and others, produced the extremely detailed, highly coloured *hokukai* batik, using Japanese-inspired patterns and aimed at a Japanese market. These *tulis* batiks provided much work but required only a small amount of cloth, for they were so complex that a single cloth could take up to two years to complete.

After World War II came the nationalist struggle, led by Sukarno, against the Dutch attempt to return. During this period of chaos, batik production suffered in particular, starved as it was of imported cambric. Independence was achieved in 1949, and Batavia, the capital of the Dutch East Indies, became Jakarta, the capital of Indonesia. In the 1950s there were rebellions against the central government in both Sumatra and Sulawesi, the Sulawesi uprising culminating in the depopulation of those hill districts in which the Toraja wove their striking warp-ikat cloths. Much was then lost, and only inferior cloths have been woven since. In Java itself, the royal courts lost their hitherto great powers of patronage, to the detriment of fine *tulis* work. The resulting void, though, has been imperfectly filled by patronage from the governing elite and rich but often undiscerning tourists. Courts on the outlying islands also gradually lost their powers, with the consequent diminution of both the quality and number of textiles woven.

In Java, a cotton-manufacturing industry was set up and machine-printed imitation batiks became common. Developments over the last twenty years include both the introduction of screen-printing and the use of batik techniques to create vivid pop art paintings. Since 1970 the screen-printing of batik patterns, which is both speedy and cheap, has become very popular. Batik painting, an art form imported from Singapore and Malaysia, is very much in vogue in Jogjakarta. The incredible growth of Bali as a popular tourist centre, pioneered by some itinerant Australian surfers in around 1970, has engendered a large export-orientated textile industry. Much of the cloth is batiked with colour often painted or sprayed on. The workers are mainly Javanese, and impatient Western buyers often have to await their orders while everything stops for the monsoon or the Muslim fasting month of Ramadan.

Most of the fine textiles of Indonesia have been produced by women. The men undertake some workshop and factory production, and make textile tools, such as metal stamps or wooden looms, but all the steps in the creation of cloth, from the preparation of the ground, the planting of the cotton and the gathering of the dye-plants to the final weaving of the patterned fabric, are traditionally exclusively undertaken by women. Great care is taken in the different processes of textile production – clarity of pattern and precision of weaving add to the intrinsic value of the cloth. Many of the processes involved are both time-consuming and labour-intensive.

Weaving is so widespread across the country that it has become almost synonymous with the Indonesian identity. Indeed, those areas such as Irian Jaya, where weaving is not practised, are culturally at odds with the Indonesian mainstream. Given the tropical climate of the archipelago, clothing requirements are actually relatively meagre, and garments are simple, traditionally composed just of rectangular cloth. There are four main types: *kain*, which wraps around the waist and legs; sarongs made of a smaller *kain* sewn into a tube-shape; *selendang* breast and shoulder cloths; and *selimut*, large wrap-around mantles of blankets. But textiles have a ritual significance that far exceeds utilitarian need, and this accounts for the great number of cloths used and produced over and above the requirements for everyday clothing.

To this day, Indonesian life is dominated by a belief in the presence of ancestral spirits who can influence, for good or ill, everything from the very times of day to the vital labours of weaving and harvesting, and the important religious rituals that ensure fertility, health and power. Indonesians see the universe as a spiritual realm comprising an upper world of gods and deified ancestors and an aqueous lower world of crocodiles and lizards, of earth and fertility. Mankind lives in between these worlds and must strive to maintain a harmonious position between them. To this end, the spirit world must be propitiated or interceded with, especially at certain crucial periods of particular vulnerability, such as birth, first hair-cutting, the filing down of the incisor teeth (without which a favourable rebirth is believed impossible), circumcision, marriage and death. At these times the soul-force of the individual needs strengthening, and gifts given at the rites of passage conducted by the extended family are the material means of channelling the aid of spiritual forces to the person at risk. Gifts from the husband's side of the family are classed as 'male' and will include money, weapons and animals. Gifts from the distaff side are 'female' and will consist overwhelmingly of textiles. Textiles thus play a vital role in maintaining harmony and balance between spirits and humanity.

The use of these ritual cloths is particularly prevalent amongst what textile scholars Warming and Gaworski call the 'ancient peoples of the archipelago', encompassing, amongst others, the Bataks, the Toraja, the Iban Dyaks, the Sumbans, the Timorese, the Nias islanders and the people of the Kroe-Lampung region in Sumatra. Some of the most striking textiles of the archipelago were created by the 'ancient peoples' for ceremonial use, often to define a ritual area, and motifs symbolizing death can appear in these cloths. Birds representing the soul are worked into the textiles of Timor. The long, narrow *palepai* supplementary-weft cloths of south Sumatra depict a 'ship of the soul' on a voyage, and in Lampung these were hung behind a person undergoing a period of life crisis, as were the smaller square *tampan* ship cloths. The Toraja of Sulawesi wove very large warp-ikat cloths of striking, usually abstract designs and vividly contrasting colours, which were draped over a corpse or used to form an enclosure for a widow in mourning. The Toraja also made ritual use of long banners called *sarita*, which were made in simple daubed batik, or else imitated in block print of Dutch manufacture. These were hung from the gables of clan houses and from tall bamboo poles at important funerals, and were worn as sashes and turbans by shamen. *Sarita* are still wrapped around the heads of wooden effigies of the dead that are such a feature of Toraja-land.

Texiles often play an essential part in death rites. In Sumba a dead king may be swaddled in numerous *hinggi* mantles, which act as shrouds. These may depict the wealth, food, and domestic animals that are required on both the soul's journey and entry into the next world. Similar rites are practised on Timor where the corpse is wrapped in so many textiles that it loses recognizable form. Textiles can also proclaim a man's clan and family so that he will be able to join his kin in the next world. A common design on Sumban *hinggi* is the tree of skulls representing the display of trophy heads outside the king's doors. Most directly connected with head-hunting were the large warp-ikat or *sungkit* supplementary-weft cloths woven by the Iban Dyaks of Sarawak. Although they had ritual significance for less bloodthirsty concerns such as fertility, in which they were used to form large enclosures, their prime role was connected with the head-hunting deemed necessary to re-establish the correct cosmic order, thus ensuring fertility. To this end Iban head-hunters would first prepare for a raiding party by sleeping under a charged cloth, to acquire power. After the raid, women would carry the severed heads in one of these cloths and then the head-hunters would softly chant songs to their gruesome trophies.

The ritual use of textiles is not confined to the 'ancient peoples', however, nor to the outlying islands. In Bali, *lamak*, long, narrow banners of woven cloth or palm-leaf, are hung from tall poles or temple entrances for a variety of ceremonies. The sacred double-ikat *geringsing* cloth woven at Tenganan Pegeringsingan village are used all over Bali for weddings, first hair-cutting and tooth-filing ceremonies. By no means all the ritual cloths have to be specifically woven for ceremonies. Imported *patola* cloth is used to decorate temples in Bali and scraps are burnt to release its magical properties. Though it was reserved for the ruling class, and hence forbidden as everyday dress for commoners, in Java *patola* could be worn by bride and groom on their wedding day, allowing them to be nobles for the day. Analogous to the use of cloth in other islands to define a ritual area, it is the custom at Javanese and Sumatran marriages to decorate a high-canopied bed of state with all manner of textiles. In Java, batik textiles are sumptuously spread on and around the bed, and in Sumatra there is a similarly ostentatious display of *songket* brocaded cloth. It is hoped that this will be an augury of fertility and wealth.

Indonesia is changing fast in the late twentieth century. The cultures of the ancient peoples are still strong, but prolonged contact with the outside world is bound to have a detrimental effect, which will most probably be reflected in a lowering of the quality of their textiles. The Indonesian heartland is now firmly within the orbit of the rest of the world, and has resulted in more machine manufacture and less hand-production of textiles. But for all that, Indonesia will again absorb and transmogrify as it has done previously. The long tradition of textile appreciation will continue. It is still part of an upper-class Javanese girl's education to learn the rudiments of batik, as much for the qualities of patience and appreciation of aesthetics as for the learning of the skill itself.

A *sarita* banner block-printed in Holland in imitation of batik and used for ceremonial purposes by the Toraja of Sulawesi.

1   *Kewatek nai telo* three-panel dowry cloth from Lembata, made from hand-spun cotton and locally gathered dyes. The warp-ikat patterns portray manta rays that are hunted from open boats.

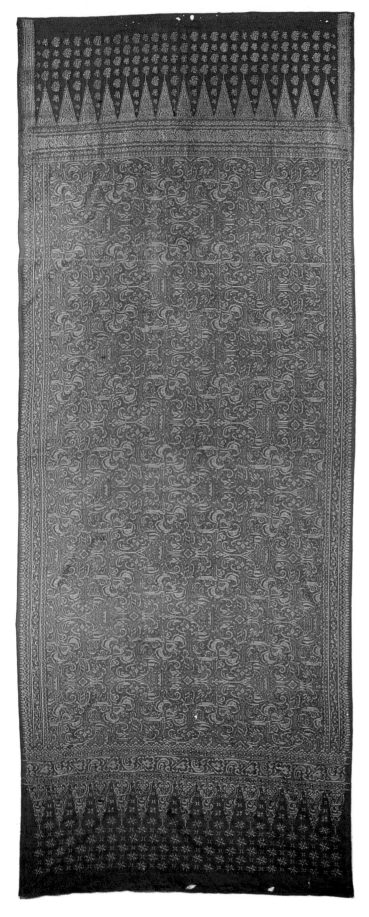

3   Double-ikat silk *patola*, woven in Gujarat, north-west India for export to Indonesia. It is worked in the *chhabdi bhat* eight-petalled lotus pattern known as *jelamprang*. This motif, and the rows of triangular *tumpal* at the bottom border, have been a pervasive influence on textile design and are found in batik and ikat all over Indonesia.

4   *Tampan* cotton supplementary-weft ritual hanging, from Kalianda district, south Sumatra.

2   A *kain limar* is worn at circumcision ceremonies in southern Sumatra. Woven at Mentok on Bangka Island, it has a silk weft-ikat field and borders of *songket* supplementary weft.

5   (Opposite) Fragment of weft ikat, woven from Chinese silk yarn in a floral pattern at Palembang, Sumatra.

6   Man's *hinggi* cotton mantle from east Sumba. The cloth is decorated in warp-ikat using vegetable dyes, with lateral stripes of royal deer, horses, birds, fish and a central *patola ratu* pattern.

7   Figures of riders on elephants, derived from Indian *patola* cloth, and indigenous motifs of men and crayfish decorate this warp-ikat *hinggi* from east Sumba.

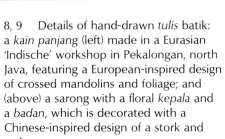

8, 9   Details of hand-drawn *tulis* batik:
a *kain panjang* (left) made in a Eurasian
'Indische' workshop in Pekalongan, north
Java, featuring a European-inspired design
of crossed mandolins and foliage; and
(above) a sarong with a floral *kepala* and
a *badan*, which is decorated with a
Chinese-inspired design of a stork and
rushes.

10   (Opposite) Naturalistic designs of
birds and flowers are set against a
background of Delft tiles on this *tulis*-
work sarong from north Java.

11 Batik altar-cloth for a Chinese shrine, made in Cirebon, north Java. Motifs are of Chinese lions and clouds.

12 Designs of birds and foliage are worked in couched metal-thread embroidery inset with mirrors on a baize background. This hanging is intended for a bridal 'bed of state'. Malay peoples, north-east Sumatra.

2   Yarns, Looms and Dyes

The raw materials from which the impressive range of Indonesian textiles are created are mainly indigenous to the archipelago. Cotton has been widely cultivated in the islands for at least two thousand years – in the fifth century AD ambassadors to Sumatra returned to the Chinese court with examples of cotton cloth, which was then little known in China. A range of dyes from locally available plant and mineral sources enabled the Indonesians to achieve colours of a depth and variety scarcely rivalled in other parts of the world. Cotton, silk – the silk moth *Bombyx mori* was first reared in Sumatra more than one thousand years ago – bast fibres and, lately, machine-spun synthetics are dyed either with traditional vegetable dyes or else commercially with chemicals. They are woven into fabrics patterned in ikat, or with supplementary warp or weft decoration, on locally made backstrap or frame looms.

Yarns

Cotton

Certain strains of the *Gossypium* cotton genus are probably indigenous to the Indonesian islands. Varieties such as the short staple *Gossypium herbaceum* and the shrub-like *Gossypium arboreum* are grown as subsistence crops on many of the outer islands, particularly in the Nusa Tenggara chain. These plants are raised either in the corner of a rice field or vegetable garden, or else planted between rows of maize or other field crops. The cotton plant takes six months to reach maturity, and the tropical monsoon climate provides ideal conditions for cultivation – a wet spell during initial growth followed by a long, dry period whilst the plant matures.

Up until the nineteenth century Indonesia was self-sufficient in cotton, but Dutch plantation policy, with its emphasis on the forced substitution of cash crops for locally consumed produce, swiftly led to a steep decline in the domestic production of cotton. Since that time, the shortfall in domestic supply has been made up with massive imports of Indian and American cotton. The Indonesian government, though, since Independence, has attempted with some measure of success to make Indonesia self-sufficient in cotton by means of the commercial cotton plantations that have been started in north Sumatra, Lombok, Flores and Sumbawa.

Many hand-woven Indonesian textiles now use machine-spun thread bought from a local store, but some thread is still hand-spun out of locally grown cotton. To prepare the thread by hand, the raw cotton must be dried and cleaned and then put through a gin made from a wooden frame inset with two wooden rollers. These rollers are each geared at one end so that they interlock. By turning a handle attached to one of the ungeared ends, the rollers are made to rotate in opposite directions. The cotton is then fluffed up using a rattan-stringed bow, to make the fibres light and airy and easier to spin. Next the cotton is laid out on a flat stone and formed into cylinders of convenient size by rolling a spindle over it. The cotton is then spun using either a drop spindle or a type of spinning wheel introduced by the wartime Japanese. With both methods of spinning a leader of yarn must be teased out of a bundle of cotton. The drop-spindle consists of a wooden spindle rod attached to a weighted whorl. The spindle whorl is

A border of browsing deer from a supplementary warp-decorated sash, east Sumba.

25

spun by hand as it rests on a base such as a sea-shell or an old Chinese porcelain bowl, while the fibres are pulled out against the twisting length of yarn. In the case of the spinning wheel the first leader of yarn is knotted on to a horizontally mounted spindle shaft. The spindle is turned by means of a connecting belt or string attached to a wooden wheel. By spinning the wheel with one hand, slowly at first, the fibres are fed on to the spindle with the other, so that the spun thread collects on the spindle.

Silk

The silk textiles of Indonesia are associated with the courts of the various islands and are renowned for their range of colours and fineness of patterning – a result of a complex series of dyeing and weaving processes. Silk yarn was largely imported from China, though silk cloth would have been imported mainly from India (*sutra*, the Indonesian word for silk, is of Sanskrit origin). Silk has been cultivated intermittently on Sumatra since the times of the Srivijaya Empire. The knowledge of the process of rearing the silk moths most probably came from mainland South-East Asia. Silk, unlike cotton, is an ideal fibre for textile manufacture. In its cultivated form it has length and elasticity, is strong and even in diameter, fine to the touch and absorbs dyestuffs of all kinds with ease.

The larvae of the silk moth live on the leaves of mulberry trees and pupate by secreting the gum sericin and a cocoon of very long silk fibre, which is often a kilometer or more in length. Cultivated silk worms meet their death at the end of the cocoon stage before they have a chance to eat their way out through the fine fibrous cell which confines them and turn into moths. The dormant larvae are dropped into a cauldron of boiling water so that the entire length of the silk filament is preserved. Much of the sericin is dissolved by the boiling water, and the remainder of the gum is removed after the filament has been wound, or alternatively after the cloth has been woven. Today there are two centres of sericulture in Indonesia: a small experimental project at Paya Kumbuh in west Sumatra, and the village of Tanjucu in south Sulawesi, which supplies the Bugis silk industry in Sengkang.

Other Fibres

The bark of the paper-mulberry tree is used to make ritual and working clothes in parts of Sulawesi and Kalimantan. On certain isolated Indonesian islands with little or no locally available cotton, thread manufactured from bast or leaf fibres was used to weave cloth. The two most notable examples are *abaca* (*Musa textilis*) and *lemba* (*Curculigo latifolia*). *Abaca* is a wild banana plantain and is found on the Sangihe and Talaud islands to the north of Sulawesi and on Mindanao in the Philippines. The outer leaves of the plant are pruned of any non-fibrous pulp and then passed through a toothed stripper. The results of this process are long silken threads known locally as *koffo*, which are then knotted end to end to form yarn. *Abaca* fibre accepts dyes well and the finished *abaca* textile is often polished with ashes and shell to give it a becoming sheen. Fibre made from the leaves of the *lemba* plant – a wild grass found in Borneo – is used by the Benuaq tribe of the Mahakam River area of east Kalimantan to weave warp-ikat cloth and was also once used by the Dusun tribe of Sabah, north Borneo.

On the Tanimbar islands, to the east of Timor, warp-ikat cloth is woven out of threads from the *lontar* palm (*Borassus flabelliformis*). The Toraja of Sulawesi once wove ritual clothing out of pineapple fibre, and thread taken from the *pandanus* and *sago* palms is still used in some parts of east Indonesia.

Looms

Indonesian looms are of two basic types: the backstrap body-tension loom, used all over the islands for the domestic production of cloth, and the shaft frame-loom, which

1. Heddle up

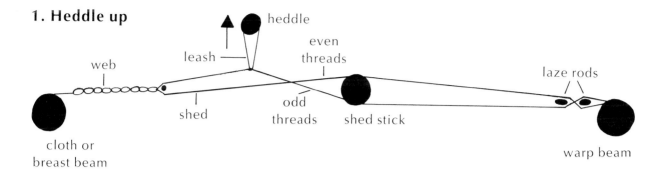

2. Heddle down

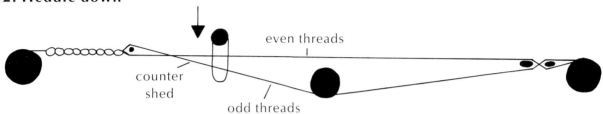

is associated with the courts and used for commercial workshop weaving. As is customary, the menfolk will make or provide all the materials and build the loom, but the women will then take over all stages of cloth production. And, with the exception of large-scale commercial production, it is the women, too, who will take the cloth to market and sell it.

Body-tension Looms

The backstrap body-tension loom is a very simple mechanism, on which some of the finest ikat and most complex supplementary warp and weft fabrics are woven. Frameless, its essential elements consist of a breast beam and a warp beam that are joined together by the warp threads, and a belt with a back-rest made of wood or hide, which is tied to the breast beam. The warp beam can be attached to any convenient pole or tree. The weaver sits with legs outstretched on the floor or ground with the belt around her waist. By bracing herself against this backstrap she is able to keep the warp threads stretched out before her under the required tension. By leaning backwards or forwards she can tauten or slacken the warps at will.

The body-tension loom has many advantages. It is cheap to make, can be easily set up, and then rolled up and stored away when not needed. No special weaving shed is required; the loom is simply erected in the shade of a tree or, more commonly, underneath a stilted house. There are two ways in which warp can be set up on a backstrap loom, continuously or discontinuously.

The warp threads of a discontinuously warped loom can either be cut and tied individually to both warp and breast beams, or more commonly the warp threads can be wound back and forth around warp and breast beams without a break. In the latter case the top and bottom sets of threads are woven together to form a single piece of fabric that stretches from one beam to the other. To ensure stability the warp beam is

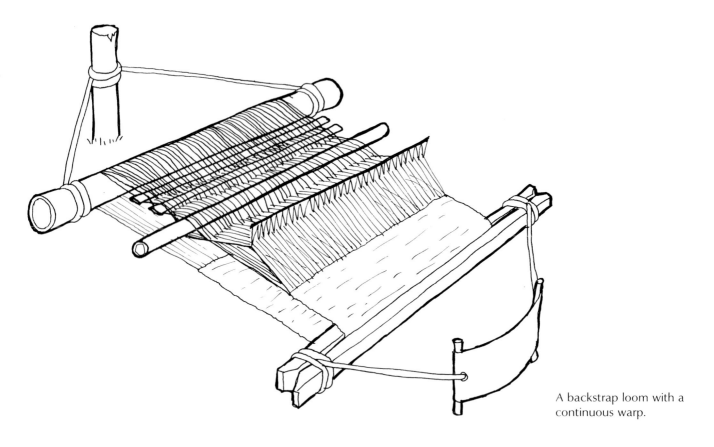

A backstrap loom with a
continuous warp.

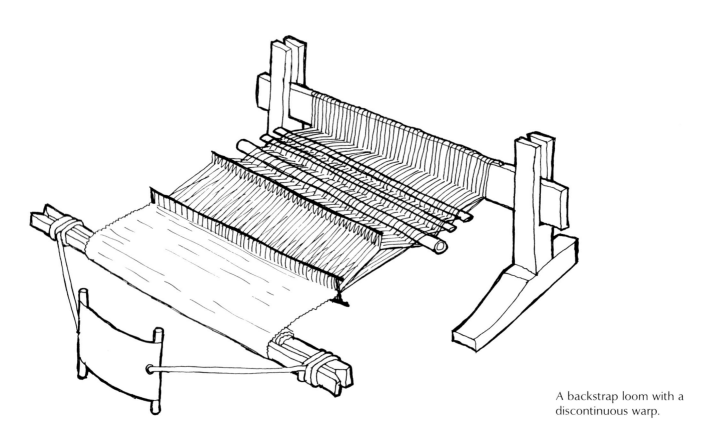

A backstrap loom with a
discontinuous warp.

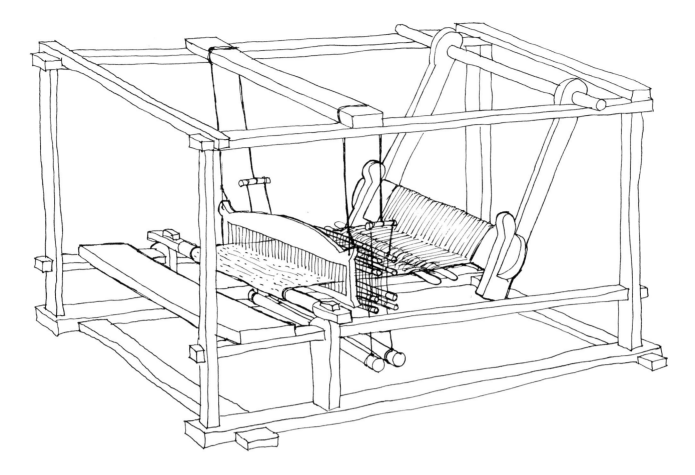

A Malay counter-balanced shaft loom.

set in heavy, often ornately carved, wooden supports. A discontinuously warped loom is much less restricted in the length of its warp than is the continuously warped loom, since any excess length of warp may be wrapped around the warp beam and let out as weaving progresses. In a like manner the cloth, as it is woven, can be wrapped around the breast beam.

Continuously warped looms are used all over the archipelago for weaving plain or warp-ikat patterned sarongs, *selendangs* and *selimuts*, whose dimensions have always been defined by the limited lengths of cloth that can be woven on this type of loom. The warp threads are in this case again wound back and forth around warp and breast beams but the length of the finished cloth is restricted by the length – and hence the weight – of warp that the weaver can easily bear against with her back. Only the threads on the topside are woven together, by the raising and lowering of adjacent threads with the aid of a string heddle rod and a shed roll. As weaving progresses the newly woven cloth is moved around and underneath the breast beam so as to bring more unwoven warp threads from the underside around the warp beam and on to the top side of the loom. To prevent the cloth from slipping during weaving, the breast beam often has a piece of wood of similar shape and size attached to it to clamp the cloth in place. This clamp can be untied to release the cloth when it needs to be shifted round. With both continuous and discontinuous warp looms the width of cloth woven is rather narrow, limited as it is by the arm span of the weaver. Cloths wider than about 60 cm (2 ft) are usually made up of two or three strips of narrow cloths sewn together.

Malay Shaft Looms
Counter-balanced shaft looms are used in Indonesia to weave fabrics for the royal courts and for the commercial market. Their main use is for weaving *songket* supplementary weft cloth. In Indonesian Kalimantan, Sambas, north of Pontianak, and Samarinda on the east coast produce a great deal of fine work with floral and geometric

motifs on sturdy Malay shaft looms. Shaft looms are also used at neighbouring Mukah and Kuching in Sarawak, at Brunei Darussalam, in Sumatra, Java and on the Malayan peninsula.

The working parts of the loom are suspended from two lateral beams which run across the top of a sturdy wooden box-shaped frame about 120 cm (4 ft) high. A bench is set into one end of the frame for the weaver to sit on. From there she can operate with her feet the transverse treadles which are connected to the heddle rods lying above the warp threads. In its simplest form, there are two treadles connected to two heddle rods. These heddle rods are in turn attached to two small wooden rods suspended above them at the sides of the loom, so that when one treadle is depressed, this brings down one heddle rod, tilting down at one end the small wooden rods to which it is tied and raising the same rods at their other ends and thus the other heddle rod. In this manner, depressing alternate treadles raises and lowers alternate heddle rods to create shed and counter-shed. From the same cross-beam is suspended a wire-toothed comb-like reed which is used to beat in the weft. From the crossbar furthest from the weaver are slung two J-shaped wooden supports in which rests the plank-shaped warp beam.

Fly-shuttle looms

A semi-mechanized loom known as the A.T.B.M. was introduced into Indonesia by the Japanese during World War II and is used for the commercial weaving of weft ikat and other fabrics. The weaver (often male) tugs down on a cord attached to a pulley, shooting across the cloth a boat-shaped shuttle containing a bobbin of the weft thread. The advantage of the A.T.B.M. loom is that it allows greater widths of cloth to be woven and increases the speed of weaving.

Dyes

Most Indonesian textiles are decorated by the processes of resist-dyeing. Indeed, the art of resist-dyeing is so widespread across the archipelago that the local names of batik, plangi, ikat and tritik have now been adopted internationally as generic terms. Aniline dyes first introduced in the 1880s are common in factory production, but natural dyes are still very much in use for the painstakingly crafted textiles worked in the outlying isles of the archipelago. Natural dyes are either substantive or adjective. Substantive dyes can fix colour without the addition of a mordant, and sources include varieties of lichen, the bark and heartwood of trees and of course the indigo shrub. Indigo (*Indigofera tinctoria*) is a shrub native to South-East Asia. Historically it was of great importance, yielding many times the quantity of the blue dye agent indican than plants native to parts of Western Europe. The Dutch colonizers of Indonesia planted vast quantities of indigo and exported it to Europe. It was a lucrative trade, threatened successfully by British competition at the beginning of the nineteenth century, and lasting until the chemical components of indigo were synthesized in Germany in the 1880s. Indigo is a vat dye which requires two stages in the dyeing process. First of all, the dye compound must be made soluble in water, and then it must oxidize on the fabric. Outlined below is the traditional process of turning the insoluble indigo dye agent indigo blue into soluble indigo white, which adheres to the dip-dyed cloth and on being taken out of the dye vat reacts with the air and turns the cloth blue.

To dye blue a coconut shell full of natural indigo is added to a water-based solution of lime and molasses sugar, traditionally contained in a wide-mouthed glazed earthen-ware pot but nowadays in a concrete vat. The mixture is stirred and left till the following morning when it will be ready for use. Through fermentation the sugar transforms the insoluble indigo blue into soluble indigo white while lime turns the solution alkaline. Sometimes the sap of the tingi tree (*Ceriops candolleana*) is added as a fixing agent to

The royal family of Livemata, Amarassi District, Timor, clad in loincloths that have been patterned in warp-ikat with locally gathered dyes.

accelerate the process. Other ingredients such as chicken flesh could also be added in order to propitiate threatening evil spirits. Light shades of blue can be obtained by soaking cloth in an indigo dye bath for a few hours. For darker shades the cloth needs to be dip-dyed approximately ten times a day for at least six days. A black colour can be achieved by repeated dyeing with indigo, or alternatively by overdyeing a dark indigo blue with brown. With the advent of naphthol and indigosol chemical dyes, dyeing cloth blue can now take only a few minutes. Racks on pulleys are positioned above the dyeing vats to lower the cloth in and out of the dyeing solution. The cloth is then dried in an adjacent courtyard. In Java the processing of indigo dyestuffs and the actual dyeing are always the work of the men.

Morinda citrifolia (turkey red, *mengkudu* or *kombu*) is one other famous Indonesian traditional dye. The dye-bearing morinda tree has its origins in the Middle East and was brought to the Indonesian isles via India. Its roots, which contain alizarin, are pounded and mixed with water. To this mixture are added the crushed leaves of alum-bearing plants such as the *Syplocos* genus. Alizarin is an adjective dyestuff which needs to react with a mordant such as alum in order to dye threads a range of reds.

A crucial step in the dyeing process is the pre-soaking of threads in oil; in east Nusa Tenggara *kemiri* candle-nut oil is commonly used. This prevents the subsequent addition of the mordant alum from drying on the cloth and crystallizing. In order for the right shade of red to be achieved, this process is repeated up to thirty times in one day. Blue and red are always dyed cold. Browns are obtained from a variety of sources. The bark of the *soga* tree (*Peltophorum ferrugineum*) which is still widely used today has always provided the brown shades so characteristic of central Javanese batik. Other shades of brown can be obtained from the tingi tree. Green is produced by overdyeing a light indigo blue with yellow.

Other common sources of natural dyes are sappan wood (*Caesalpinia sappan*), safflower (*Carthamus tinctorius*), turmeric (*Curcuma longa*) and the jackfruit tree (*Artocarpus intiger*). Dye from the heartwood of the sappan tree yields a bright red

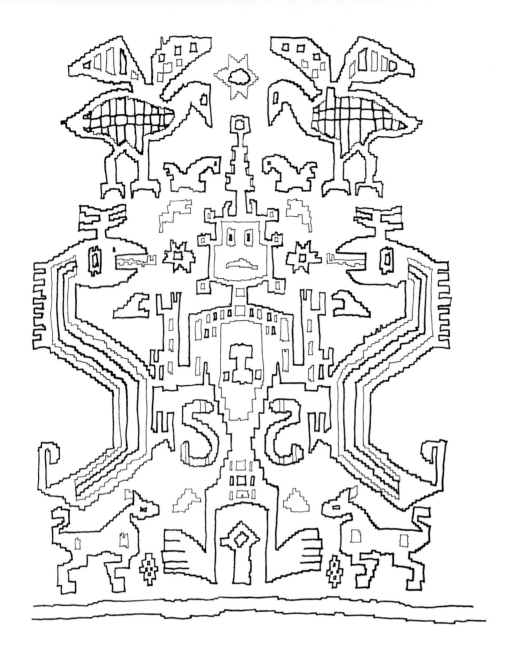

Warp-ikat rendition of a man, Chinese-inspired dragons, snakes, animals and birdlife, from a man's *hinggi* mantle, east Sumba.

colour when applied to mordanted fabric. From safflower is obtained a fugitive yellow. A crushed boiled paste of turmeric root also yields fugitive yellow but can be combined with other substances to give oranges and browns – the Iban of Sarawak use it as a component in their red dyeing process. The jackfruit tree is grown all over South-East Asia and is valued both for its fruit and its hardwood timber. Boiled jackfruit wood chips provide another source of yellow dye.

The delicate shades and subdued colours of the traditional batiks of Java largely resulted from the restricted range of natural dyestuffs available and the tendency of these naturally derived colours to fade in strong sunlight. The locally available dyestuffs in each area produced strong regional colour characteristics in the batik of what used to be isolated areas until the developments made in transportation in the late nineteenth century. In commercial cloth production, nearly all these natural dyes have now been supplanted by chemical substitutes, and the introduction of synthetic alizarin and indigo, along with aniline and auramine dyes, has destroyed distinction of colours from the different regions. Chemical dyestuffs are coming into increasing use on the outer islands, particularly in places like east Sumba, which has an export market for its traditional warp-ikat *hinggi* mantles. But where textiles are still being woven for home consumption, dyes are still painstakingly gathered from local plant life and prepared by women under conditions of secrecy (with certain ritual taboos) to produce the warm soft colours so beloved of the islanders.

13 (Opposite) Toraja woman weaving cotton *lurik* cloth on a body-tension loom, Sa'adan village, south Sulawesi.

14   Warps and a partially woven section of a supplementary-warp sash, Pau village, east Sumba.

15   Woman winding yarn on to a bobbin for weft work, Prailiu village, east Sumba.

16 Bobbin of weft thread in a wooden shuttle, Sukarara, Lombok.

17 (Right) Half section of a contemporary Iban warp-ikat *pua*, with realistic designs of head-hunters, from Sarawak.

18 Weaving a supplementary-warp patterned *selendang* on a body-tension loom in Pau village, east Sumba.

19, 20   Hanks of weft yarn tied with resists of plastic twine (detail, left) and ikat-tied weft threads on a frame ready for dyeing, in Sukarara, Lombok.

21   *Mengkudu*-dyed warp threads drying on a pole, in Prailiu village, east Sumba.
22   Freshly dyed weft yarn drying on racks, in Sukarara, Lombok.

24 (Top) A *tulis* batik-worker waxing in the resist with a *canting*. Trusmi village, Cirebon, north Java.

25 (Above) Printing batik yardage with a *cap* copper stamp, Jogjakarta.

26 A classical dancer of Jogjakarta, dressed in a batik *kain panjang* and a batik *patola*-imitation waistcloth.

23 (Left) The stages of batik (a description of each is given on p.44).

27 A selection of *canting* – the waxing instrument used to draw out *tulis* batik – each with a different number of spouts.

29 Two men wearing *tulis soga*-dyed batik waistcloths, Jogjakarta.

28 *Cap* copper stamps from central Java, seen here both from the front and back, featuring a *sawat* design based on the mythical bird Garuda's wings.

30 Waxed cloth being dipped into a dye bath in a batik workshop, Jogjakarta.

31 (Right) Batik cloth drying on racks after dyeing, Jogjakarta.

33　Two palace attendants wearing batik waistcloths and headcloths, Jogjakarta.

32　*Tulis*-work *kain panjang* from Cirebon, with patterns of Chinese clouds and the *kraton* palace gates.

3   The Decorative Craft of Batik

Batik is the most renowned textile art of Indonesia and the technique itself – applying a wax resist before dyeing to form a pattern in negative – is known world-wide by this Malay name (meaning to draw with a broken dot or line). Batik is also practised in India, China, South-East Asia, Turkestan, and West Africa; but in Indonesia, on the island of Java, the craft has been brought to an acme of refinement. Nowhere else has wax-resist cloth been so finely detailed, and one has to go back to the beautiful seventeenth- and eighteenth-century painted chintzes of the Indian Coromandel Coast to find anything that can rival Javanese batik for subtlety of colouring and mastery of the dyeing processes.

There is much scholarly dispute as to the origins of batik. Was the art brought by traders from China, where there is early evidence of the use of wax resists for patterning cloth? It is more probable that it came from India, which had a renowned textile tradition, and which, from the second to the fifteenth century, had exerted a most profound influence on the religion and culture of Sumatra, Java and Bali. Excavations at Fostat near Cairo have yielded evidence of the early use of wax-resist techniques on fourteenth-century trade cloths from Gujarat, on India's west coast. Indonesia's hot, damp, tropical climate, however, combined with the fragile and perishable nature of cloth itself, has meant that the oldest surviving example of Indonesian batik cannot be dated before the latter half of the eighteenth century.

The first actual mention of the word 'batik' occurs on a Dutch bill of lading of 1680 pertaining to a shipment of cloth from Batavia bound for Bencoolen. But not until the early nineteenth century did Sir Stamford Raffles, governor of the Dutch East Indies during the brief period of British rule, write the first detailed account of the batik process. It was the Javanese invention of the *canting* waxing instrument that without doubt enabled fine hand-drawn batik to be worked, however. Fine, smooth cloth is required for this *tulis* (literally 'writing') work, otherwise the spout of the *canting* will snag. Those scholars who point to the Indian origin of batik argue convincingly that for this very reason, *tulis* work was only possible on fine imported cloth that came from India before 1800, and from then on increasingly from the Europe of the Industrial Revolution. The corollary of this argument is that batik is an art that developed quite recently in Indonesia, in the eighteenth and nineteenth centuries, growing in scope and sophistication with the increasing availability of imported cloth. The simplest and ritually most significant of Javanese batiks are the *kain simbut* cloths of Banten, west Java, on to which a rice-paste resist has been applied with a bamboo splint, and a cold *mengkudu* dye solution brushed. When this paste has been removed by soaking the whole fabric in cold water, a design of an empty central lozenge is revealed, in white, surrounded by a large number of mystical and magical symbols all set against a red background.

The batik work of central Java is mainly produced around the courts of Jogjakarta and Surakarta and is characterized by the use of *soga* brown and indigo blue dyes. Batik is one of the five fine *halus* arts of Javanese civilization: women of the *kraton* courts had the leisure to create the most beautiful patterns mainly based on flowers and foliage. The patterns were, however, rather conservative, reflecting the splendid but politically impotent roles the central Javanese courts played throughout the Dutch colonial

Floral batik border from a north Javanese sarong.

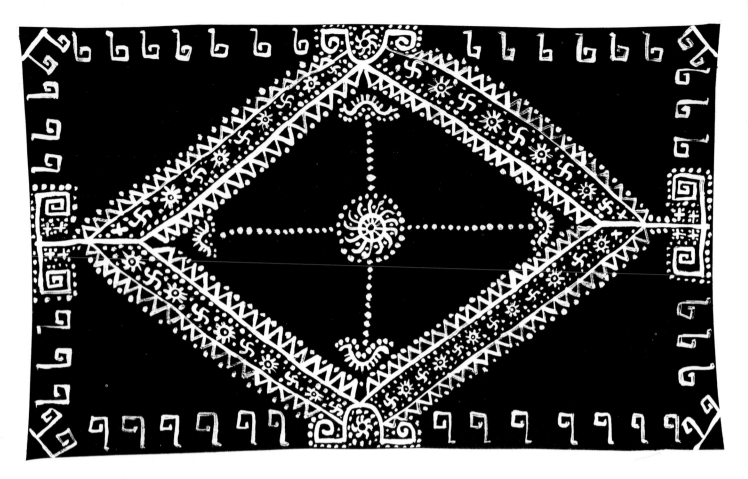

Kain simbut ritual cloth from Banten, west Java, decorated with magical motifs in rice-paste batik.

period. The working of batik by the ladies of the court was not only a pastime but also a valuable source of income, as many of their courtier husbands would have been unsalaried. Running in parallel with this *kraton* batik was batik as practised in the surrounding countryside. In the quite periods of farming life, when they were not involved in planting and harvesting, women would produce simple batik for home use or for sale at local markets. The last survival of this art is at Kerek, an isolated village near Tuban in eastern Java.

The dynamic mixture of cultural influences that centred around the north-coast ports of Java produced the sometimes gaudy splendours of north-coast batik between 1840 and 1940. North-coast entrepreneurs were innovative and pioneering, deriving designs from such diverse sources as Chinese mythology, Arabic calligraphy and even European horticultural books. Ateliers of Pekalongan district, such as that of the Chinese Oey Soe Tjoen, were amongst the first to experiment with the new aniline dyes coming from Germany at the end of the nineteenth century. Floods of European machine-printed copies of indigenous batik patterns had started arriving in Java in the 1830s. In response, Chinese- and Arab-owned workshops were set up to produce batik that was printed with a *cap* stamp rather than hand-drawn with a *canting*. The batik process thus became faster. Twenty batik cloths a day could pass through a factory, whereas before, with the *tulis* method, a cloth would take a month or more. The Javanese preferred *cap* batik to imported machine-printed cloth, as it was made of better quality material, was cheaper and longer-lasting, colourfast and of a pattern more attractive to local eyes. Javanese *cap* batik stemmed the flood of imported foreign textiles and its own export markets were set up on the other Indonesian isles.

Four grades of cotton are used as batik base cloth. *Merah* is the coarsest, then, with increasing fineness of weave, comes *biru*, *prima* and *primissima*, the finest and most tightly woven cloth. The preparation of this cloth is traditionally a man's task. The length of cloth to be batiked is first hemmed and then boiled to remove any starching matter. The cloths are then soaked in peanut or castor oil; this helps the dyes to penetrate the fibres more deeply. By boiling the cloth in an alkaline soda bath any excess oil can be removed, and after drying the fabric is stiffened, using rice or cassava starch.

The women who create *tulis* hand-drawn batik often first draw out guidelines on the base cloth or copy a pattern directly from an old batik. An experienced worker, though, will often work from memory. Care is taken not to make mistakes, since large errors can only be retrieved by boiling out all the wax and starting again. The cloth to be batiked is laid over a rack known as a *gawangan*. Groups of women sit on small stools or mats around a centrally placed basin known as a *wajan* which is filled with melted wax and kept at a constant temperature by placing it on a small brazier known as an *anglo*. The *canting* is held between thumb and forefingers, the cloth in the left hand. The batik worker fills her *canting* bowl by dipping it into the *wajan* and, holding it horizontally to prevent spillages after first blowing gently through the *canting* spout to clear any blockages, starts waxing out the design by tilting the *canting* slightly forward in flowing lines just above the surface of the fabric. A *canting* with a single spout of very small diameter is used for finely detailed work. If a very large area has to be blocked off, a cotton wad is attached to the *canting*, or a stick is used. Multiple spouts draw out parallel lines or dots. Tiny dots can be created in the pattern by pricking areas of wax resist with a *cemplogen*, which is a set of needles mounted on a wooden handle.

Using a combination of *cap* (block-printed) and *tulis* (hand-drawn) work, a design of a peacock and foliage has been worked on this *combinasi* batik *kain* from central Java.

Three women from central Java, each using a *canting* to draw out batik designs in wax on cloth, prior to dyeing.

Batik wax is a mixture of different proportions of beeswax and paraffin wax, to which resin and animal fats may be added. The beeswax comes from the islands of Sumatra, Sumbawa and Timor, and renders the batik wax more malleable – a high percentage of paraffin wax will make batik wax brittle, resulting in a crackled, veined and marbled design, esteemed in the West as a hallmark of batik but looked down on in Indonesia as inferior workmanship. For a completely crackled effect pure paraffin is brushed on to the fabric. Pine resin and eucalyptus gum both have a high melting point and are added to the resist to promote adhesion. Animal fat, however, has a low melting-point, is easy to remove and gives the resist greater flexibility.

For quality batik, the resist is always applied first to one side of the cloth and then the other, the outlines on the first side acting as a guide to help the worker reproduce the pattern exactly. The completion of a piece of batik involves a series of stages of waxing and then dyeing, waxing fresh areas of the cloth, taking off some portions of the first waxing and then dyeing in another colour. The more complex the desired colour scheme, the more stages there are.

Batik in central Java is usually dyed in two colours, and requires two types of wax, to be applied before the dyeing process starts. The first application of wax is called *klowong*, and this must be brittle enough to scrape off easily after the first dyeing. The second is called *tembokkan* (literally 'wall'), and is applied to those parts of the cloth that are to remain uncoloured by any of the succeeding dye baths. *Tembokkan* wax must not crack when the cloth is being dyed, and must be sticky enough to adhere well – but not so sticky that it makes the *tembokkan* wax difficult to remove at its final boiling out. The brittle *klowong* wax has less eucalyptus, less fat and more paraffin; the darker, more flexible *tembokkan* has higher proportions of beeswax, resins and fats. The various stages of batik are depicted in illustration 23 and are as follows: **a** the first application of wax, *klowong*; **b** the second application of wax, *tembokkan*; **c** the first dyeing (blue), *medel*; **d** the first wax removal, by scraping, *negerok*; **e** the third application of wax, *mbironi*; **f** the second dyeing (brown), *menyoga*; **g** the final removal of wax, by boiling, *nglorod*.

The *cap* method was introduced using copies of European stamps in the middle of the nineteenth century. Workshops were then set up and men hired to undertake the arduous and unhealthy work. The iron-handled *cap* stamps are built up out of thin strips of copper with upright strands of wire set in to print dots. Each *cap* usually makes up an entire design unit. Those of a symmetrical pattern element can be used on either the top side or the reverse of the cloth. For a non-symmetrical design element, an image for the top and mirror-image for the reverse of the cloth is needed. Large design elements may be split up into smaller component *caps* for ease of handling.

Cap printers stand at tightly padded-out rectangular tables. Beside them on a small stove sits a circular flat-bottomed pan containing the wax. A filter made of a percolated copper plate and a fibrous mat is set in the molten wax and covered with an absorbent cloth. Any impurities in the wax are strained out by the filter. The *cap* is pressed on to the filter pad and then stamped on to the cloth. The worker repeats the process to leave imprints of the design all over the cloth; changing *caps* as the design requires, he continues until the whole cloth is covered with wax. *Cap* workers are paid by the piece so work is swift.

Indonesian batik has a vast repertoire of designs derived from natural and mythical sources, from indigenous folklore and from the waves of foreign culture that have engulfed the archipelago. The many batik designs fall into one of three categories: geometric designs; non-geometric, figurative designs; and background designs, known as *isen*. The most commonly used geometric designs are called *ceplokan*. These designs are forms of flora, fauna and bird life standardized into geometric shapes. Other popular geometric patterns are the *garis miring*, diagonally slanted designs of which the *parang rusak* (broken knife) and the *udan liris* (light rain) are the most famous. *Kawung* designs – groups of ovals arranged in fours – are also classed as geometric, as are the *tambal*

Block-printing a design with a copper *cap* in a batik workshop in north Java.

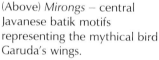

(Above) *Mirongs* – central Javanese batik motifs representing the mythical bird Garuda's wings.

(Right) A cockerel motif rendered in batik with a *cap* metal stamp, central Java.

miring (patchwork) and the *tumpal* (spear) designs. Patchwork is considered to have magical properties: the Sultan of Jogjakarta, for example, possesses a famous magical patchwork jacket which is worn on important ceremonial occasions. The *tumpal* appears on Indian trade textiles but would also seem to be an ancient indigenous design.

Semen (non-geometric) designs are patterns of swirling foliage, combined with stylized depictions of birds, animals and mythological figures derived from indigenous Javanese, Indian, Chinese or European sources. Common motifs are variations on the theme of Garuda, the mythical winged hybrid mount of the Hindu god Vishnu. Many, too, are variations of the Chinese phoenix. Subaqueous creatures are often-used *semen* designs, as are butterflies and bees and Chinese-inspired lions and *nagas* (dragons, or snakes) which symbolize fertility and the female, watery underworld. *Megamendung* Chinese cloud designs and ground-plans of Chinese rock gardens are worked in layers of graduated colour in Cirebon. The concept of clouds ready to burst is potent with sexual imagery. Mountains are a recurring theme of Javanese batik and are said to symbolize Mount Meru, which lies at the centre of the Buddhist world. The *alas-alasan* forest design is another notable *semen* pattern.

Isen (background) designs are simple, repetitive motifs which, in the plainest, least expensive batik, can cover the whole surface of the cloth. The Chinese-derived swastika or *banji* is an important *isen* motif. The oldest patterns are naturally of Javanese origin, notably *gringsing* – the fish-scale motif – clusters of dotted semi-circles which are traditionally worn to ward off illness.

Regional Styles

Central Java   Central Java is considered to be the home of batik. Central Javanese batik is itself conservative in nature, and orientated towards – and indeed often worked within – the confines of the *kraton* palaces of the sultanates of Jogjakarta and Surakarta. Central Javanese batik is worked in three colours, indigo blue, *soga* brown and shades of white. In Jogjakarta batik is worked on a clear, bright, white background, in contrast to Surakarta, where the background colour is cream. Much *tulis* batik is still produced in the tiny workshops within the confines of the *kraton* at Jogjakarta, and this, with the larger *cap* and *tulis* workshops to the south of the *kraton*, forms the core of Jogjakarta production. Jogjakarta is also the centre for batik painting, an artform imported from Singapore and Malaysia in about 1970.

Textile production in Surakarta is much more dynamic. It forms the nucleus of most of the large Indonesian batik concerns, such as Danar Hardi and Batik Keris and a substantial proportion of this factory batik is exported to neighbouring countries. Surakarta still produces fine *tulis* work, however, with much of the first waxing painstakingly worked over a period of months by women in such outlying villages as Wonogiri and Byat before the cloth is sent to the large factories for dyeing.

South-West Java   The batik of south-west Java is mainly produced in and around the towns of Tasikmalaya and Banyumas, whose designs are based on central Javanese styles. Tasikmalaya is the home of the Obay Hobart concern, which produces quality *tulis*-work shirt-pieces, and in Banyumas fine *parang* designs are created using *soga* brown, golden yellow and bluish black.

The North Java Coast   Although the trading ports attracted Arabs, Europeans and Chinese in great number, with the exception of the Muslim sultanates of Cirebon and Demak there was little court life on the north coast. There thus arose an unstratified, thrusting, dynamic polyglot society, which was looked down on by the conservative courts of central Java. There were, however, cultural contacts between the north coast and central Java, and intermarriage took place between aristocratic groups (one of the consequences of which was the transfer of skilled batik-making workers from the *kratons* of central Java to the north coast). From the 1830s on, the Dutch began exporting to Java large quantities of Dutch- and Swiss-produced, machine-printed batik imitations, and with the great increase in the Javanese population encouraged by Dutch plantation policies a large market for such cloth was created. All this imported cloth was manufactured from American cotton, but due to the outbreak of the American Civil War there occurred a long hiatus in the import of printed cloth. To fill this gap in the market Chinese, Arab, Eurasian and European entrepreneurs began to set up factories producing both *cap* and *tulis* batik. Women *tulis* workers were lured out of their homes to practise their craft in the new workshops.

Due to the outward-looking nature of the north-coast people and the absence of restrictive sumptuary laws, the palette of north-coast batik was extremely varied, ranging from bright reds and yellows to traditional blues and European- and Chinese-inspired soft pastels. The Chinese, the Eurasian 'Indische' and the Arabs were the three main entrepreneurial groups on the north coast. The most noted of the Indische entrepreneurs were J. Jans (known as 'Widow Jans') and Mrs Eliza Van Zuylen, whose working life spanned the heyday of north-coast batik. Mrs Van Zuylen established a workshop in Pekalongan in 1890. Her whole family was involved in the business, the women setting up the designs and organizing the labour whilst the men supervised the dyeing of the cloth, finance and the retailing of the finished product – the sexual division of labour that still holds good in the batik industry today. Indische designs were derived from such varied sources as Dutch horticultural books, magazines and even postcards, and Indische entrepreneurs were responsible not only for the introduction of new

Two boys wearing sarongs worked in *tulis* batik on handwoven cloth at Kerek village, Tuban District, north Java.

Chinese bird motif from a *lokcan* silk batik *selendang*, from Cirebon, north Java.

colour combinations but for changes in the basic layout of the sarongs produced as well. The Indische women were the first to sign their batiks, and were noted for their use of soft pastel colours produced from natural dyes.

The Chinese, on the other hand, were the first to use chemical dyes in the making of batik. Aniline dyes were available in Java from around 1890 and naphthol dyes from 1926. By the mid-nineteenth century a strong Chinese entrepreneurial class was already very well established on the north Java coast. Each coastal city had its own Chinese quarter, with Chinese shops and temples. The Chinese were deeply involved in batik manufacture in this early period, for sale both to their own community and to outsiders. Batik made for their own community was colour-coded according to the age of the wearer. Young girls would wear light blues and pinks, middle-aged women blue and red, and the older generation a selection of green, blue, brown and purple set against off-white. *Selendangs*, used as baby slings all over Indonesia, were red, the Chinese colour of good luck.

The Arab community had a preference for *jelamprang* and *ceplokan* patterns based on *patola* designs worked in Islamic green. Arab manufacturers were particularly predominant in Gresik. There, and in Demak, Kudus and also Cirebon the *kalligrafi* prayer shawls and headcloths were made, inscribed with Islamic symbols and quotations from the Koran. Much of this production was exported to Jambi and Palembang in Sumatra.

Ceribon: Ceribon, with its two *kratons*, Kanoman and Kasepuhan, was a great centre of the arts and was both a base for the dissemination of Islam and a place of major Chinese settlement. Due to thirteenth-century guild prohibitions against women becoming painters or artists, the men, rather than the women, made the *tulis* batik of Ceribon. Consequently, the Ceribon style of batik is very different from elsewhere in Java, vigorous in form, eschewing extraneous detail, with bold motifs set against a clear background. Production today is centred on nearby villages such as Weru and Trusmi, which have the reputation for making some of the finest contemporary batik. Ceribon patterns are deeply influenced by Chinese art.

Indramayu: Now reduced, almost, to the status of a fishing village, Indramayu was once famous for introducing its own particular style of batik, distinguished by the restrained use of shades of *mengkudu* red and dark indigo blue. Motifs were inspired by local marine life, and at Indramayu, as at Lasem, a technique was developed to fill in background space with pin-like dots.

Pekalongan: Pekalongan is popularly known as 'Batik City': indeed, a large proportion of its heterogeneous population is involved in the business of batik. Some of the finest batik comes from the Chinese in the nearby village of Kedungwuni or from Javanese women in the surrounding *kampungs* (hamlets). Pekalongan was home to the ateliers of the famous Indische batik-makers, and still claims many famous Arab and Chinese batik concerns. Pekalongan batik-makers were the first to experiment with chemical dyes, and the first *cap* batik was made here. Traditionally Pekalongan batik was produced in shades of pinks, blues and yellow but the introduction of chemical dyes that can be quickly and simply used has extended the colour range so much that almost any colour combination can be expected. The multicoloured batik favoured in Pekalongan, if dyed by traditional means – even with fast-acting synthetic dyes – involves an arduous and painstaking process. To speed up the process and to exploit the properties of the synthetic dyes successfully, a technique originally imported from India known as *coletan* is used. An outline of the motif is first drawn out in wax, and the dyes are then painted directly on to the enclosed space. The coloured motifs can thus be entirely sealed off with wax, on both the top and reverse sides. The cloth can then be dip-dyed in the background colour.

Lasem: Lasem, once a great north-coast port, is now a shadow of its former self. Between 1870 and 1942, Chinese concerns in Lasem conducted a booming business in *cap* and *tulis* batik. The most characteristic feature of Lasem batik was its deep blood-red colour, unobtainable anywhere else. Today there are still a few *tulis* workshops in the compounds of the high-walled Chinese houses. Batik in the *tiga negri* ('three-country') pattern is now a popular design.

Juana: Juana was the centre for the manufacture of silk *selendang* shawls, batiked with Cirebon-inspired *lokcan* designs on Shantung silk imported from China. *Lokcan selendangs* in black or brown, on a cream or blue background, are worn for ritual and festive use both in Bali and in the Minangkabau areas of Sumatra. Due to the scarcity of silk, *lokcan* production has now steeply declined.

Tuban   Village batik still survives around the main north coast and central Javanese batik production areas, but village women act almost exclusively as outworkers for the batik companies of the cities. A notable exception can be found in and around the isolated village of Kerek, near Tuban, east Java, where a range of *tulis kain* and sarongs are decorated with designs of mostly Chinese inspiration, drawn out on hand-woven cotton cloth. The colouring, whether indigo blue, synthetic red or more recently *soga* brown, is indicative of status and, as a general rule, the darker the colour of the cloth, the more prestigious the person who wears it.

Madura   Madura lies north east of Surabaya between Java and Bali; a long, arid island populated by tough seafarers and farmers, it has a centre of distinctive batik-making at Tanjung Bumi on its north-west coast. All Madura batik is *tulis* work, the majority being quite roughly drawn in the Tuban tradition, but with some fine work both chemically and naturally dyed. In contrast to Java, it is not blue that is the first dye to be used, but red. Rather than dip-dyeing, colour is applied to the base cloth with a scrubbing brush; thus colouring tends to be rather pale.

Sumatra   Two important centres of batik-making outside Java are those of Jambi and Palembang in south-east Sumatra. Much influenced by the imported block-printed cloth from India, production in Jambi and Palembang was originally orientated towards the courts, and used Indian-style wooden blocks for printing. Headcloths and prayer shawls featuring Arab calligraphy and Islamic motifs were drawn out in *tulis* work in Jambi and although this has now died out, *kalligrafi* cloths are now made in Bengkulu and some *tulis*-work is still done in Jambi and Palembang.

Prada
Gold leaf dust or paint can be applied to batik and other fabrics to produce luxury cloth for wear at festivals and religious ceremonies. The gold pigment is applied only to one side of the fabric, creating a splendid visual effect but with economical use of an expensive material. In central Java, Chinese gold leaf is applied with albumen to such ceremonial cloths as the *kain dodot*. On the north coast of Java gold dust is used and glued on with a mixture of albumen or linseed oil mixed with yellow earth. In both areas the gold colouring applied usually follows the layout of the existing batik patterning. Alternatively, in Bali, the gilding can be laid out to form independent motifs over the original batik, creating a startling new pattern. Gold leaf dust was here stuck on with a fishbone glue, though now, as in the rest of Indonesia, tubes of bronze paint are used (usually Winsor and Newton paints imported from England). Today in Bali, in Satria and other villages around Klungkung, bronze pigment paints are applied to cheap, brilliantly coloured synthetic materials to form religious banners (*ider-ider*), parasols, breastcloths and skirtcloths. The same technique is used to embellish batik in central and north Java and even plangi and tritik in Palembang, Sumatra.

Detail of a cotton *prada* cloth decorated with gold pigment, with patterns of birds and flowers. From north Bali.

A Balinese temple dancer wearing a golden headdress and body jewelry, and clad in a *prada*-decorated skirtcloth.

34   (Opposite) *Cap* block-printed batik *kain panjang* from Surakarta, in the *parang* pattern. The *soga*-brown and indigo-blue colour combination is typical of central Javanese batik.

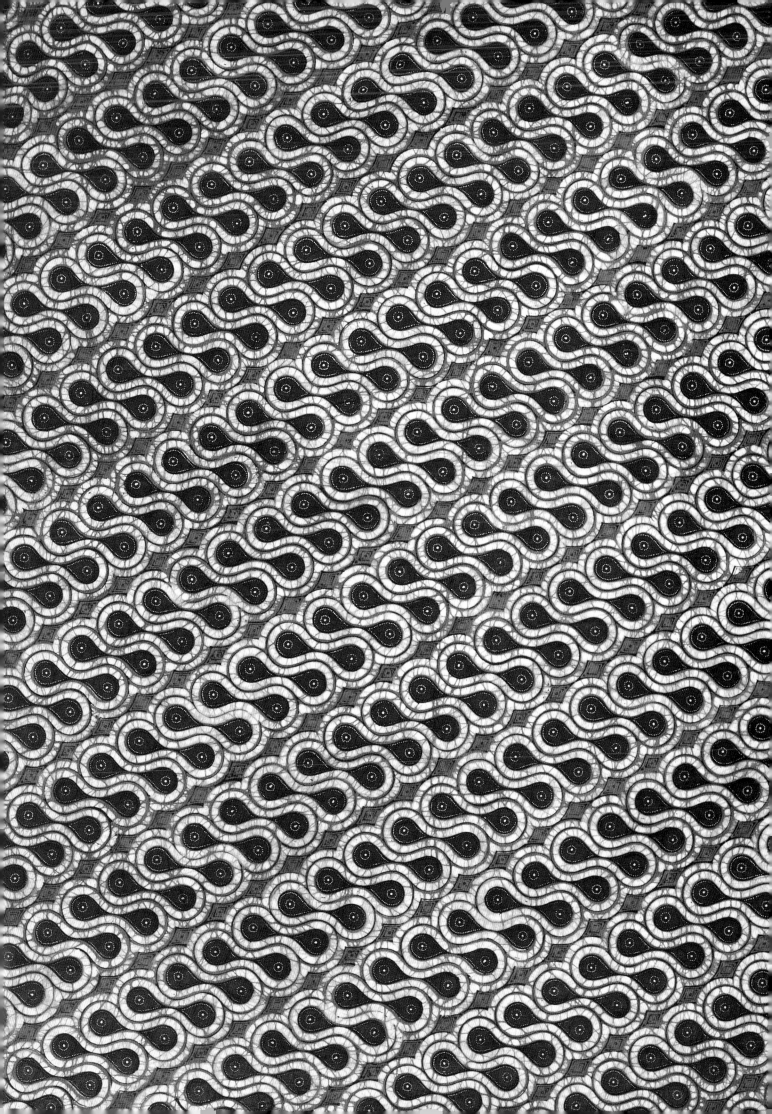

35 Detail of a *tulis*-work sarong from Pekalongan. The patterning of flowers, foliage and birds is combined with floral borders that are a north Javanese innovation.

36 (Opposite) In this *tulis* batik *kain* cloth from Pekalongan, motifs of storks and reeds are set against the *parang rusak* design that originates in central Java. *Parang rusak* was a proscribed design restricted to royal use in central Java, but on the north coast such restrictions were ignored.

37   (Opposite) Motifs of flowers and foliage are worked in *tulis* batik on this *kain panjang* from Tanjung Bumi, Madura Island. The colours are applied with a brush.

38   Section of a *tulis kain panjang* from Trusmi village, Cirebon, in the *taman arum* design of Chinese rock gardens, trees, lions and mythical beasts.

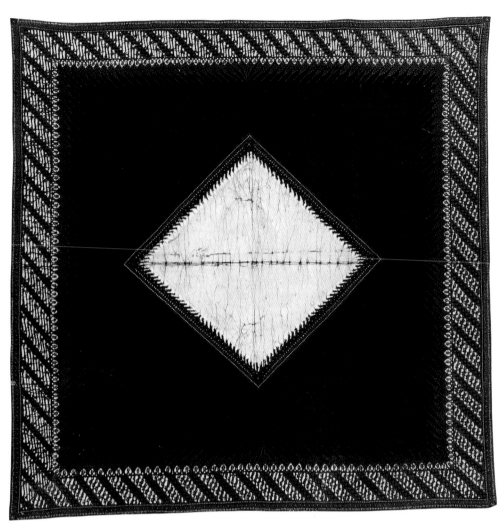

39 Cap-printed *iket kepala* headcloth from Surakarta.

40 Detail of the *kepala* and *badan* of a *tulis* sarong from Pekalongan, worked in the blue shades preferred by the Chinese.

41 Muslim man's headcloth drawn in *tulis* batik in the *kalligrafi* pattern based on Arabic verses in the Koran. From Cirebon or Jambi.

42 Detail of a sarong from Pekalongan or Lasem, with a *tulis* batik pattern of birds and foliage inspired by the painted chintzes of India's Coromandel Coast.

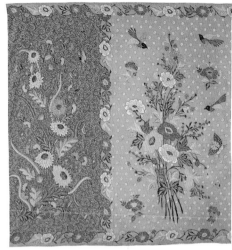

43, 44 *Tulis* batik sarong (above) from Pekalongan, north Java, with a floral *kepala* (left), worked in the light blues and pinks favoured by the Chinese community. Many such patterns were taken from Dutch horticultural books or magazines.

45, 46 Finely detailed floral pattern in *tulis* batik typical of the workshop production of Oey Soe Tjoen in Kedungwuni.

47 Batik *selendang* from Pekalongan, decorated with figures of Chinese dragons and lions. It is used as a baby sling, and details are painted on in the *coletan* process, waxed over and then over-dyed in red, the Chinese colour of good luck.

48 *Pagi-sore* (morning-evening) batik *kain panjang* from the north Java coast. The differently patterned halves can be alternated – one side is worn outermost during the day, the other in the evening.

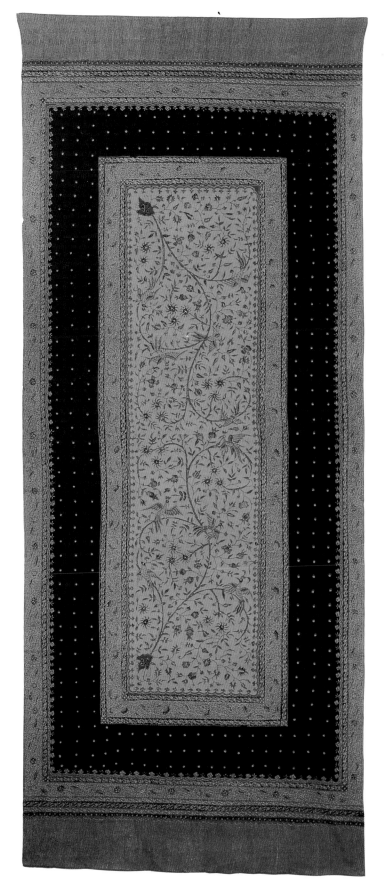

49 Contemporary *tulis* batik *selendang* with Indian-influenced layout and design. Made in Cirebon for the Sumatran market.

50 *Tulis kain panjang* from Cirebon in the *megamendung* Chinese cloud design.

51   *Combinasi* (*tulis* and *cap*) batik *kain* from Jogjakarta, with details of batik motifs outlined in *prada* goldwork.

52   (Opposite) Detail of a *kain dodot* from central Java. This is a very large textile for ceremonial wear. The area surrounding the central lozenge is decorated in *prada*.

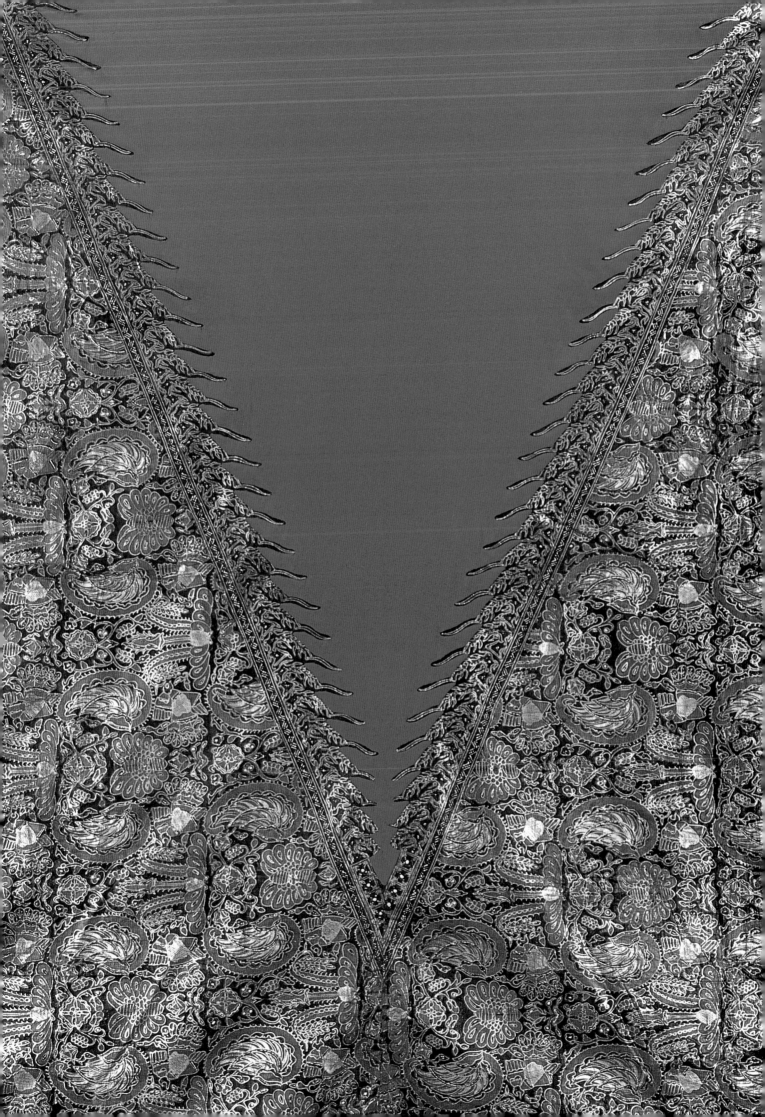

53 Detail of a *cap* batik *kain panjang* featuring repetitions of the *jelamprang patola*-inspired design produced around Surabaya for the Arab community.

54 Market women wearing *cap*-batik *kain* waistcloths and *selendang* shawls in Jogjakarta.

55 *Lokcan tulis*-batik sarong worked in Shantung silk in Juana, north Java, for festive use in Bali.

56 Detail of *tulis*-work *kain panjang* from Lasem, with Cirebon-influenced designs of Chinese phoenixes and foliage.

Oei Kling Liem

57   Detail of a signed batik by Oe Kling Liem, a
Chinese batik-maker from north Java. The Chinese batik
workshops of north Java were the first to experiment
with aniline dyes. In this case the dark background dye
proved to be fugitive.

58   (Opposite) *Tulis* batik, again by Oe Kling Liem. The
pattern of birds and flowers and the floral borders in
pale pastel colours are typical of north-coast batik.

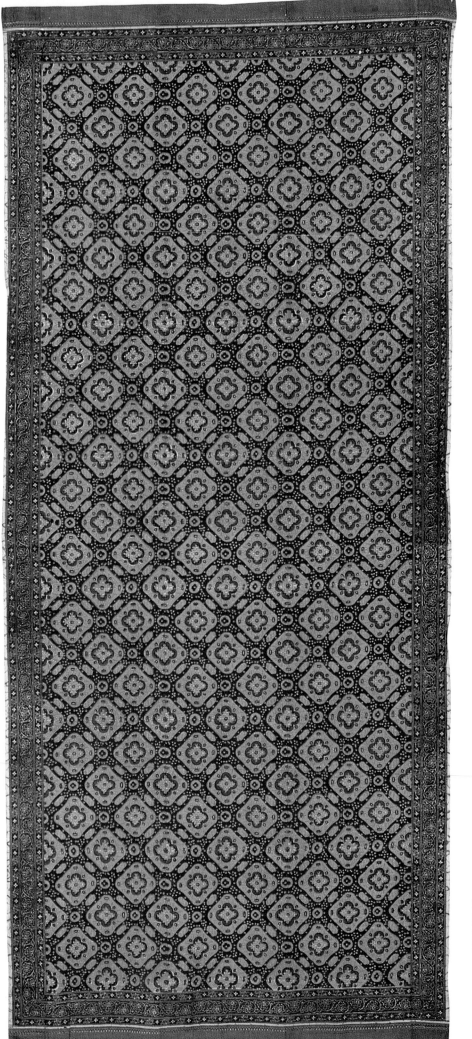

59　*Selendang* from Jambi, *cap-*printed in imitation of Indian trade textiles from the Coromandel Coast.

60 *Cap*-batik *selendang* from Jambi. Wooden printing-blocks were often used in Jambi rather than copper ones.

61 (Far left) *Kemben tulis*-batik breastcloth from Pekalongan.

62 (Left) *Selendang* with *lokcan* designs worked in *tulis* batik and *soga* dyes on hand-woven cloth, from Kerek, near Tuban, north-east Java.

63 (Above) Indigo-dyed batik *pipitan* skirtcloth or shouldercloth from Kerek.

64 (Opposite) *Putihan* batik sarong from Kerek. Thrice-dyed indigo, it is for use in ritual by an old woman of high standing.

65 Woman wearing a *cap*-batik *kain panjang* examining bolts of cloth in the Pasar Klewer cloth market, Surakarta.

66 (Right) *Cap*-batik *selendang* in the *parang* design, from Surakarta.

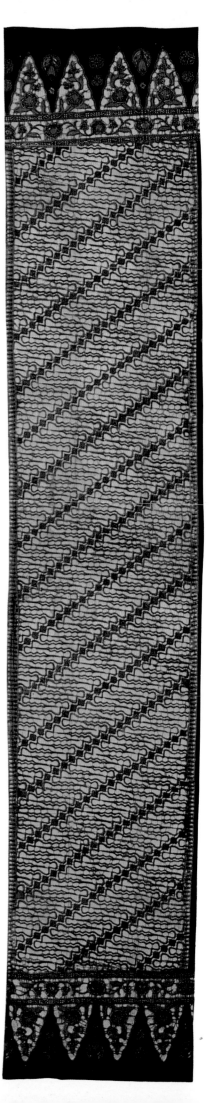

67 Very finely detailed *tiga negri* (three-country) *tulis*-batik sarong started in Pekalongan. The blue was added in another north-coast town before the cloth was *soga*-dyed in Surakarta.

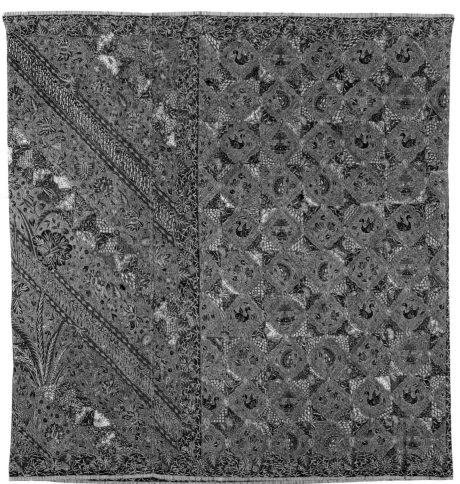

68–72 Details of *tulis*-work batik sarongs from Pekalongan. The background of the *badan* (top) is worked in one of the oldest batik designs, the *grinsing* fish-scale motif. The *kepala* (top right) of a very fine *tulis* sarong in the *dua negri* (two-country) style combines work from Lasem (the deep red) with that of Pekalongan, whereas the example at centre right has an Indian-influenced pattern of a peacock on a bush. European-derived motifs of flowers and birds are worked in the bottom cloths.

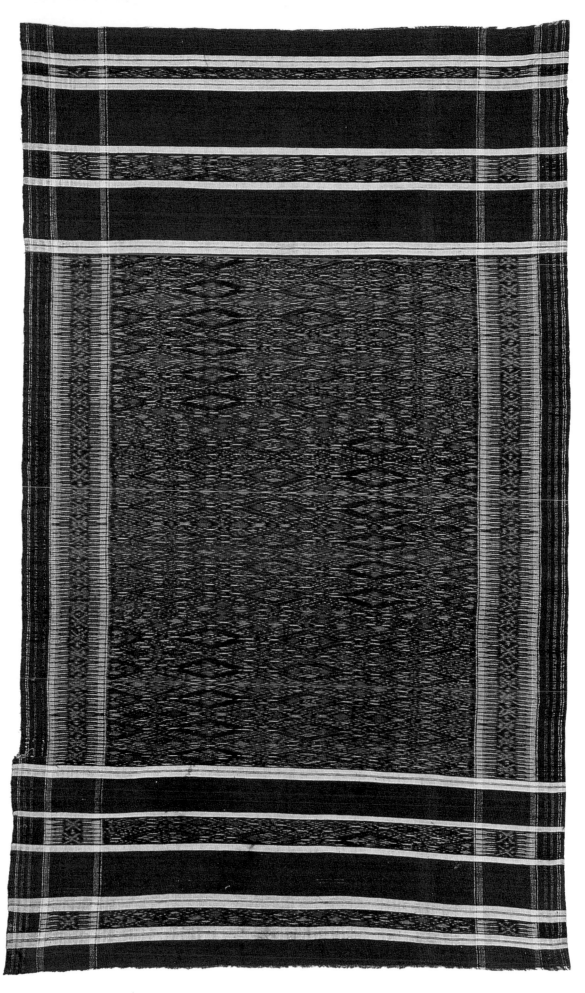

73   *Cepuk* cotton weft-ikat ritual textile, with *patola*-inspired designs from Nusa Penida Island, Bali.

4   A World of Pattern

In addition to wet rice cultivation and bronze-casting, the Dong-Son culture also introduced to the Indonesian islands the technique of weaving warp-ikat textiles on a simple backstrap loom. Warp-ikat cloths are the textiles most characteristic of Indonesia, as warp-ikat weaving has been practised on nearly every island of the archipelago.

The word 'ikat' is derived from the Malay word *mengikat* (to tie, or to bind) and is a method whereby the patterning of a textile is obtained by tying fibre resists tightly around the warp threads and then immersing the tied hanks in a dye bath. The pattern obtained is akin to a photographic negative (if, for example, the original thread is white and the dye bath blue, the tied portions form a white pattern against a blue background). By tying up further sections of the warp threads, untying certain sections of the originally tied resists, and then immersing the tied hanks in a dye bath of a different colour, a pattern emerges that is of four colours, the first of which being the original undyed colour of the warps. Those warps left untied on the first dyeing and then tied to protect them from the second dye bath take the colour of the first dye, usually indigo blue, and those portions tied to protect them from the first dye bath, then untied to allow the second dye colour to penetrate, take the colour of the second dye, usually red, traditionally *mengkudu* (*kombu*) derived from the roots of *Morinda citrifolia*. The fourth colour is the colour obtained from the mixture of two dye baths, usually black (the mixture of indigo blue and *mengkudu* red). This affects those sections of the warp threads left untied for both dye baths to penetrate.

The basic ikat technique can be applied either to warp or to weft threads alone. Alternatively, certain sections of the textile can be warp ikat, such as the borders, and other parts weft ikat – the body, for example. The most complicated ikat of all entails the dyeing of both warp and weft threads by the ikat process. Once woven together, these form a cloth of complex patterning known as 'double ikat'. Ikats are usually woven on simple looms in plainweave (warp-faced for warp ikat, weft-faced for weft ikat, and balanced weave for double ikat). The ikat technique can be applied to any fibre that will take up dye – cotton, silk, wool, bast or hair. For climatic reasons warp ikat is almost always tied on cotton, or occasionally bast, in the isolated outlying islands. It is traditional, however, for weft ikat to be worked in silk.

Patola

One of the great influences on a variety of Indonesian textiles is the *patola* silk double ikat from Gujarat in north-west India. These textiles, which came to be known as *cinde* in Java and Sumatra, were brought to the Indonesian islands in the fifteenth century by Muslim traders from India's Malabar coast. The vivid patterning, soft luxurious texture and fast colours of these cloths would have formed an extremely desirable contrast to the textiles of the archipelago, which must at that time have been of rather dull, coarsely woven cotton, decorated in crude warp ikat. *Patola* became a prestigious item desired in all the courts of the islands, valued also as a ritual textile. One of the first moves the Dutch made when they began to dominate the inter-island trade was to monopolize the trade in *patola* and to grant gifts of the cloth as a mark of favour and recognition to island royalty. *Patola*, in the process, gained such prestige that its design

A weft-twined border from a warp-ikat *ulos* made by the Toba Batak, north Sumatra.

elements were incorporated into local cloths. The popular *jelamprang* motif is derived from a particular *patola* design known as *chhabdi bhat* (the 'basket' pattern), and has been incorporated, along with other *patola* elements, into the warp ikats of many of the outlying islands.

Warp ikat

Warp ikat is primarily the preserve of the 'ancient peoples', the builders of megaliths – those groups, animist in spirit, isolationist by inclination, whose legacy from the Dong-Son culture was preserved either in the rugged mountainous interiors of the main islands, or on the outlying islands. These peoples were largely unaffected by the cultural and religious changes constantly sweeping through the coastal regions athwart the great trade routes.

Women of these cultures weave sarongs and *selendangs* on backstrap looms during the quiet hours of the heat of the day, in the shelter of the recess under their stilted houses. Young girls will learn the simpler techniques on small looms, leaving the finer weaving to their mothers and grandmothers. Traditionally the colours came from a wide variety of vegetable dyes, the most valued colours coming from the scarcest dye materials.

The Bataks

The Bataks live around the Lake Toba region of north Sumatra, and are noted practitioners of the warp-ikat technique. The Batak *ulos* cloths are usually vertically striped in muted sombre colours of blues, browns and magentas, with ikatted arrowheaded patterns. The vertically striped patterns look striking as the *selendangs* are most usually worn folded and pleated over the shoulder.

The Bataks are a large ethnic group of approximately three million who farm the fertile valleys of the highlands of north-central Sumatra. They are famed for their fierce independence, for their spectacular boat-shaped carved wooden houses, and for their warp-ikat textiles. Their culture is centred around the great, still Lake Toba and the sacred island of Samosir which lies within it. The Bataks are divided into six groups who speak different but related languages. The Angkola and Mandailing to the south, who were Islamicized during the Padri Wars of the mid-nineteenth century, the Toba from the Lake Toba region, who were converted to Christianity by Protestant German missionaries from 1864 on, and to the north the Pakpak/Dairi, the Simalungun and the Karo, who are now mostly Christian, although some are Muslim. Elements of the ancient Batak religion linger on, however, particularly amongst the Karo.

Though Western-style dress is prevalent in the Batak area, especially amongst the men, the traditional *ulos* rectangular cloths decorated with simple warp-ikat or extra-weft patterns (and sometimes with both) are essential wear at weddings and funerals. *Ulos* cloths are also prescribed articles in the complex series of gift exchanges that takes place at these and other important ceremonies that mark rites of passage.

The most significant ritual cloth is the *ulos ragidup*. At weddings the *ulos ragidup* ('the cloth with the pattern of life') is presented by the father of the bride to the mother of the groom. This both emphasizes the superior status of the bride-givers and confirms that the two sides of the new family are now inextricably linked. The *ulos ragidup* is a large *selendang* with the dark borders in plainweave and a central field of warp stripes or simple arrowhead warp-ikat patterning. This is attached at the top and bottom to two sections of complex extra-weft patterning on a white background, either by sewing, or by attaching new warps to those of the central field and continuing the weaving process. The narrow borders are woven separately and then sewn on to form a rectangular cloth. The ends of the *ulos* are finished off with weft twining in fine geometric patterning.

Anthropomorphic figures from the central panel of a warp-ikat *selendang* from Niki-Niki, west Timor.

A *selendang* with the *ragi hotang* rattan pattern is given to the bridegroom and the *ulos sibolang*, a blue textile with lateral bands of warp-ikat patterning, is given by the bride-givers to the family of the groom. The *sibolang* is also an important funeral gift and is worn as a headcloth by the widow. *Ulos* may be worn as shouldercloths, sarongs or headcloths, and it is often the colour rather than the patterning that is symbolically important. White can mean purity, red bravery and black eternity. *Ulos* of blue or red are used to cover the deceased.

The centres for warp-ikat weaving are in the Porsea area on the southern shores of Lake Toba, around the village of Tarutung. Batak warp-ikat textiles are woven on horizontal, continuously warped backstrap body-tension looms. Dyes were traditionally of vegetable origin – the Batak were reputed to take up to ten years of successive dyeing to achieve the right shade of indigo and made much use of *Morinda citrifolia* – yarn having previously been soaked in buffalo fat to help the red morinda dye adhere. Patterning in Batak textiles is achieved by alternating different-coloured sections of ikat. Another method can be used after dyeing, whereby the ikat-tied sections are undone; the appropriate warp threads are then manipulated and pulled forward so that an arrowhead formation is achieved.

The weavers around Lake Toba are the sole remaining practitioners of hand-loom weaving. They can weave not only in the Toba style, but will also produce cloths in the style of the Karo, Simalungun and Angkola Batak, to be sold in their local markets.

Regional Styles

Aceh   Aceh, the fervently Islamic and fiercely independent north region of Sumatra, had great trading, cultural and political contacts with Turkey and India because of its geographical position. These contacts are reflected in its rich textile heritage. Aceh was unique in Indonesia in producing warp ikat in silk rather than cotton. Patterning was of simple arrowheads in the manner of the ritual *ulos* cloths of the neighbouring Batak. Typical colouring was of white-and-black arrowheads against a deep wine-red or purple background.

Sumba   In east Sumba are woven some of the most striking figurative ikats produced anywhere. Here, large *hinggi* mantles are woven in pairs and worn as loincloths and shoulder-wraps by the men of east Sumba. The most important weaving villages are Prailiu (just outside Waingapu), Pau (famous also for extra-warp weaving), Rende and other villages near Melolo, and Kaliuda on the south-east coast, where *hinggi* designs are in traditional lateral stripes and characteristically feature horses and cockerels.

Horses are a great feature of Sumba, having been exported as cavalry mounts for colonial armies, cherished by Sumban men, ridden at the *pasola* (a mock cavalry battle held in west Sumba in February and March), and semi-deified, as part of the Sumban horse sacrifice. Certain designs, as in other parts of the archipelago, were restricted to royalty and the aristocracy, particularly the *patola ratu* pattern derived from Indian *patola* textiles. Commoners wore clothing with simple ikat designs and slaves were clad in plain black. This situation pertained till the 1920s when the social structure started to change. Commercial factors also intervened. *Hinggis* were made for export, to sell to the Dutch resident in Java, to other parts of the Dutch East Indies and to the Netherlands itself. New designs were introduced, such as the Dutch coat of arms, taken off Dutch colonial coins. With the advent of a large tourist market in nearby Bali production has been stimulated even further, and many new and varied motifs are now being introduced.

The top and bottom patterning on *hinggi* mantles are usually mirror images of each other, but those now produced for the tourist market often have a design which can be read all the way down the textile, so the *hinggi* can be used as a hanging rather than as a

Jelamprang patola-derived motif, executed in warp-ikat on a sarong from Flores.

garment. Large monolithic figures have been introduced, and *hinggis* with extra-warp borders are now produced at Prailiu, and at Pau in particular. The patterning of *hinggis* intended for local wear, as well as that of sarongs, remains very much the same as before. The dyes used are indigo and *mengkudu* – nowadays often with some admixture of chemical dyes.

Ikat from west Sumba is much less figurative, the designs usually being of *mamuli* (the vulva-shaped metal ornament given as part of the bride-price) in white or yellow – sometimes both – on a blue or black background.

Flores   Simple ikat sarongs are woven in the Ngada country around Bajawa in west Flores, characterized by bands of blue horses on a black background. In the past, sarongs were decorated with beadwork set in patterns of lozenges. Now beadwork featuring an ancestral ship pattern is being imitated and sewn to Ngada sarongs for sale in the antique markets of Bali. The pride of Flores ikat, though – indeed, some of the finest in the world – is produced in Lio district, which lies between the towns of Ende and Maumere in the shadow of the extinct volcano, Mount Kelimutu. Production is centred on the villages around Woloworo. In Jopu are woven rather debased designs, mainly in chemical colours of blue stripes against a black and *kombu* background. Similar but finer *patola*-influenced designs are worked in Wolonjita, mostly in natural colours. In Nggela, however, are woven the finest ikat sarongs of all, displaying complex figurative patterns in natural dyes. *Jelamprang* designs are used in bands in Nggela and in Wolonjita. *Selendangs* with *patola* designs, known as *luka semba*, are also woven and are worn as shawls by male ritual leaders.

Around Ende, reflecting an Islamic influence, the non-figurative ikats produced in neighbouring Ndona and the surrounding area have a central panel with a diagonally slanted *patola* design, the colours being predominantly black and *kombu*, with a little indigo blue. In Sikka district, Maumere, with its Catholic history, produces sarongs with figurative designs of birds and animals in lateral stripes against a brown *kombu*

Human figures aboard a boat, surrounded by birds, jewelry and marine life, from a warp-ikat *selimut*, Lio district, Flores.

background. To the east towards Larantuka, ikat sarongs of much simpler geometric designs are woven.

All over Flores natural dyes such as indigo and *kombu* predominate. The backstrap looms tend to be short – the length of a woman's leg.

Lembata   Lembata, also known as Lomblen, is a small island just to the east of Flores. Its intrepid fishermen hunt whales and gigantic manta rays with hand-held harpoons from open boats. The ceremonial warp-ikat sarongs of Lembata feature motifs of human figures interspersed with symbolic manta rays, sharks and boats.

The main ikat-producing centres are situated around the coast at the villages of Lamalera, Ili Api and Atadei. Their output mainly consists of the elaborate dowry warp-ikat sarongs woven in either two or three panels and known, respectively, as *kewatek nai rus* or *kewatek nai telo*. These cloths feature *patola* elements and rows of human figures and marine life, and are coloured reddish-brown, blue-black and white. They must be made exclusively from locally grown and hand-spun cotton, and dyed with locally gathered dyes such as indigo and *Morinda citrifolia*. At weddings they are given in exchange for the bride-price of an ancestral elephant tusk, which must be provided by the groom.

Savu   Savu is a dry island of charming people that lies between Timor and Sumba. The main industries are toddy-tapping and warp-ikat weaving. Sarongs are brown, blue and sometimes a pale pink with lateral bands of either geometric motifs or European-influenced designs, such as cupids and clouds. *Selendangs* on a dark blue-black and brown background feature vertical stripes of floral and geometric designs of European inspiration. Many Savunese sarongs and *selendangs* are taken across the sea and sold in the market of nearby Waingapu in east Sumba.

One intriguing aspect of the use of textiles on Savu is the way in which different designs on ceremonial warp-ikat cloths indicate clan affiliation. There are two groups known as the 'Hubi Ae' (the Greater Blossom), and the 'Hubi Iki' (the Lesser Blossom), though membership of these groups is never acknowledged openly. The designs of each group are passed down from mother to daughter, and textiles that make exclusive use of these motifs are kept for ceremonial wear. Some mixing of designs does occur, though, on everyday clothing, but this is not seen as breaking any taboos or social conventions. The difference between the designs of the clan groups can be seen most clearly on the *selimut* men's shawls. Those of the Hubi Ae feature flower or star motifs in white, arranged in parallel vertical rows against a black background; those of the Hubi Iki depict diamond shapes, again in parallel vertical rows on a blue background.

Rote   Rote is a delightful, fertile island where toddy-tapping and the raising of beef cattle are the main industries. Previously, the womenfolk of the island wove *selendangs* and sarongs, with fine floral designs made of lozenge-shaped segments of colour against a black background. Due to cultural changes over the last twenty years, and immigration to the nearby city of Kupang in Timor, Rotenese women have virtually stopped all weaving. Now, from the tiny neighbouring isle of poor, dry Ndao, come male metalworkers and female weavers and dyers, who produce rather crude warp ikats in somewhat garish chemical colours.

Timor   The long, dry island of Timor is administered in two sections that have two different colonial histories. The west was Dutch, the east Portuguese, but both shared a common cultural background. East Timor was only decolonized in 1974, and then invaded and annexed by Indonesia in 1975. There has been armed insurrection against the Indonesian government ever since. Instability and destruction are hardly conducive to the weaving of beautiful textiles.

Whilst woven textiles in west Timor are prolific (particularly in the central section from Ayotupas to Kefa and Atambua), the eastern side also produces beautiful ikat and extra-warp sarongs from around Los Palos in the far east of the island. Large, chemically dyed *selendangs* with ikat borders come from the Maliana region and others with rather crude depictions of birds, flowers and human figures in bright chemical oranges and greens are woven around Viveke.

From Soe and Niki-Niki in the west come *selendangs* worn in pairs by men. They are identically patterned with plain cotton orange and yellow borders and a central ikat panel with intricate motifs of hooked rhombs or fantastical frogs or lizards, beloved of Timorese mythology. The top and bottom of the *selendang* are mirror-images of each other, the warp threads of each having been doubled before the pattern is tied in. The central section between these ikat-patterned areas is sometimes filled with embroidery. The women of the royal family of Niki-Niki weave an ikat *selendang* with no plain borders so that the ikat pattern stretches right across the width of the cloth. These textiles are symbols of royalty and worn at all important ceremonies.

The Moluccas   The textiles of Kisar and the Tanimbar islands in the south Moluccas feature warp-ikat patterning in the manner of neighbouring Timor. Kisar and Tanimbar are inhabited by people once notorious as head-hunters. Warp ikat is the major form of patterning for the sarongs, loincloths and *selendangs* that are the main items of clothing.

Motifs on Kisar warp-ikat cloths are of people with arms raised in prayer, birds and animals. These are laid out in bands which appear at both the top and bottom ends of the sarong. Narrow bands of the same designs, or perhaps simple spots of ikat, fill the central body of the sarong.

Warp ikat in Tanimbar was practised on either locally gathered cotton or a mixture of such cotton and *lontar* palm fibres, though imported cotton thread is now commonly used. Designs are of human figures, flags, half-moons, lozenges and Dong-Son influenced spirals. Further to the north, on the large island of Ceram, warp-ikat is

A Toraja chief with his wife and sister, in Kalumpang, Sulawesi.

combined with supplementary-warp and -weft work in a busy arrangement of geometric forms.

Java At Troso near Jepara on the north Java coast are factories that produce great quantities of rather dull, but good quality warp-ikat imitations of Torajan and east Sumban ikat cloths.

The Toraja Highlands of Sulawesi Toraja is a name of Bugis origin, meaning 'highlander', given to the different peoples of the mountainous regions of the northern part of the south Sulawesi peninsula. The Toraja peoples have consistently resisted Islamicizing incursions from the Bugis to the south (the last only occurring in the 1950s). The Toraja native religion is megalithic and animistic and is characterized by animal sacrifices, ostentatious funeral rites and huge communal feasts. The Toraja only began to lose belief in their own religion after 1909, when Protestant missionaries arrived in the wake of the Dutch colonizers.

The Toraja divide their rituals into two halves of a circle. One half comprises the eastern ceremonies (such as house-building and rice cultivation) all of which are connected with life and the rising sun. Western rituals are connected with death and the setting sun. Offerings in either type of rite are placed at the appropriate compass point in the house or compound.

Weavers in Rongkong and the Kalumpang valley region of the isolated northern Toraja lands produced large warp ikats of striking geometric patterning which they

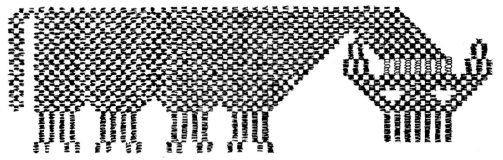

A figure of a sacrificial buffalo woven in the supplementary-weft technique at Sa'adan village, Tana Toraja, Sulawesi.

traded both to the north into central Sulawesi, and to the south into Tana Toraja, the land of the Sa'adan Toraja. In Tana Toraja two sizes of warp-ikat cloth woven in Rongkong and Kalumpang were both used in funeral rites. The *pori lonjong* (long cloth) was hung along the walls of the death house, or used to create textile pathways along which it was believed that the dead could reach the Other World. The *seko mandi*, large square cloths, were primarily used as shrouds, but could be hung as a canopy over the corpse or combined with others to create a secluded area to shelter funeral guests. The funerals of Toraja chiefs are spectacular, involving the ritual slaughter of many buffalo and mass feasting. They traditionally culminate in the burning down of the death house. Very often it is years after the death that the chief's family are able to afford such a funeral. In the intervening period the body is wrapped in many ikat and other cloths, and the widow must sit in the death house by the corpse all this time.

In the past, these large ikat cloths were used in Tana Toraja to pay fines and to act as pledges of peace between feuding aristocrats. They were made exclusively from home-grown hand-spun cotton. The dyeing process took many months. The red colouring was derived from a mixture of morinda, dammar resin and chillis. Blue came from indigo and *torae* grass mixed with ink fruit. The designs used are very dramatic arrow and triangle forms, alternating with zig-zags and the predominant hook and rhomb called *sekon*, which has been interpreted as a stylized human figure. To increase the dramatic impact of the pattern, Toraja weavers tie a double thickness of warp threads, and unusually for Indonesia, a number of women will tie the resists for one cloth. Colouring is generally blue, black and white against an apricot background, and traditionally blue weft threads are used.

The weaving centres of Kalumpang and Rongkong were decimated during the anti-government rebellions of the 1950s. Now these areas produce imitations of the old cloths for the Western tourist market, using mainly machine-spun cotton. Rongkong cloths can be distinguished from those of Kalumpang by shade of colour and layout. On old Kalumpang cloths, the component motifs filled the whole of the central field, whereas motifs on Rongkong cloths would be grouped in a central cluster with a space separating it from the borders. The black of the Kalumpang cloths is darker than the blue-black of Rongkong cloths.

North Sulawesi   Warp ikat was practised in cotton in Bentenan, north Sulawesi, with simple patterns in narrow rows, interspersed with broader bands of human figures, arms upraised in prayer, set between diamond or oval motifs. Production ceased at the end of the nineteenth century due to Christian missionary activity, which opposed any kind of expression associated with the indigenous religion.

East Kalimantan   In the Mahakam river area of east Kalimantan, the Benuaq tribe wove *bidang* skirt lengths and large warp-ikat *pua* cloths that were structurally related to Iban *pua kumbu*. These ikats are known locally as *ulap doyah* and are woven from Duan Doyo, the leaves of the *lemba* plant (*Curculigo latifolia*), a wild swamp grass. This technique is still practised at the village of Tanjung Isay, which now produces pieces for the tourist trade.

Iban woman's warp-ikat *bidang* skirt from Sarawak.

Pua Cloths of the Iban Dyaks

The Iban Dyaks were the fiercest head-hunters of Borneo. Dependent on slash-and-burn rice cultivation, their land hunger fuelled constant wars of aggression against weaker neighbouring tribes.

Iban women wove very large ceremonial cloths known as *pua kumbu* (*pua* means 'large cloth', *kumbu* 'red'). These were sometimes decorated by the *sungkit* weft-wrapping technique, but mainly by warp ikat. These *pua* and other articles of clothing, such as women's *bidang* skirts, feature abstract representations of flower and animal forms, spirits from the netherworld, anatomically exaggerated male and female figures and warriors carrying trophy heads.

The *pua* were woven for different purposes, to promote fertility, to encourage a good harvest, or to receive the trophy heads upon the return of a war party. The Iban traditionally live in long houses, which have a long common gallery where many ceremonies involving a sumptuous display of textiles take place. Ritual life amongst the Iban required the periodic taking of heads and the sacrifice of animals to promote fertility and to placate the malevolent spirits bringing sickness, disease and crop failure. Heads were particularly sought after to end the period of mourning for a dead chief.

Up until recent times, every Iban woman was a weaver. As a young girl she would start weaving a *bidang* skirt decorated with a leaf and creeper design. Later, as a novice weaver, she would attempt to weave a *pua* of a specific width. After that she would attempt wider *pua* and so on, until she reached a certain level of proficiency, then she would weave a pattern that she had seen in a dream. Iban believe in a separable soul – that is, that everything has two parts: the *tubok* (physical body) and the *semengat* (soul). During a dream the *semengat* is thought to wander out of the body, and so when a mature weaver dreams of a new pattern, she is undertaking a dangerous path that she will not leave till the weaving of the *pua* is completed. She is embarking upon the war-path of women, since weaving ceremonial textiles and head-hunting are considered perilous and parallel ventures. When the weaving is completed, she can wear the thumb tattoo of a head-hunter.

Iban weaving-patterns are passed down from mother to daughter, and the choice of motifs depends on the intended use of the cloth. Such powerful motifs as the *engkaramba* spirit figures would never be incorporated into everyday clothing, but only woven by a mature weaver for a specific ceremonial purpose. *Pua kumbu* are used to define ritual areas, after which they are believed to take on supernatural powers. During the initiation of a *manang* (shaman), for instance, he is completely covered in a *pua* as he attempts to climb over a symbolic wall of fire. A *manang*, in turn, will hang a *pua kumbu* across the door of the long house in an attempt to destroy the spirits held responsible for a domestic tragedy.

Pua kumbu are woven on a simple, continuously warped backstrap loom. Traditionally the materials used were homegrown cotton and locally available vegetable dyes, such as leaves and grasses, bark, earth, lime and fruits. What distinguishes Iban warp ikat from that of all the neighbouring Indonesian islands is that the top and bottom of *pua kumbu* do not mirror each other. As the *pua kumbu* are designed mainly to be hung rather than worn, the typical pattern of interlocking repetitive motifs runs down the whole length of the cloth. To this end, the warp threads are wound round a dyeing frame that is slightly longer than the desired cloth. The upper network of warp threads will form one side of the cloth, later to be sewn to the other side (formed by the lower network) to make up the whole. The pattern is tied in with *lemba* fibre greased with beeswax (or nowadays plastic twine). The threads are first dipped in saffron water, then immersed in a dye composed of oil, fruits and seeds pounded in salt and ginger. Only a woman who has the title 'Orang Tau Nakar Tau Ngar' ('she who knows the secret of measuring out the drugs') is capable of mixing this dyestuff. It yields a light reddish-brown colour, and needs to be exposed to the light and dew (but never rain) to fix it. The second dyeing is in indigo, which yields a blue-black

Warp-ikat *pua*, Iban tribe, Sarawak.

colour (or plain blue on those sections of the first tying that have now been untied). Red can be obtained with *mengkudu* (*Morinda citrifolia*), yellow from sappan wood and brown from a variety of tree barks. The interlocking motifs can be deciphered by the Iban and interpreted as leopards and shrews (symbols of bravery), crocodiles (protectors of the rice fields), the barong hornbill (the bringer of good omen), deer (a talisman against bad luck) and many other stylized forms.

Sarawak today is a fast-developing, well-educated state with a voracious logging industry. The white rajas of Sarawak, the Brooke dynasty, long ago suppressed head-hunting. With the coming of Christianity, there have been many cultural changes and a gradual drift to the prosperous towns. Many of the rituals for which *pua kumbu* were woven and displayed no longer take place. Instead, with the coming of tourism, there is a great demand for quickly made souvenir textiles adorned with new, non-ritualistic designs of riverboats, helicopters and, of course, head-hunters, all worked in a realistic, figurative style. Traditional weavings are now entrusted in the main to a few elderly women.

Iban Dayaks from Sarawak.

Weft Ikat

Weft-ikat weaving takes place in those parts of the archipelago that were near to the trade routes: the east-coast region of Sumatra, coastal Kalimantan, south Sulawesi, the north Java coast, Bali and the adjacent island of Lombok. With the exception of parts of Bali and Lombok, all the weft-ikat weavers are Muslims, so it may be presumed that the technique of weft ikat was brought from India to South-East Asia by Indian or Arab merchants at the start of the Islamicization of Indonesia in the fifteenth century. The preferred medium is silk, originally imported from China, but today, in commercial workshops in Java, Bali and Sulawesi, the weft ikat technique is practised on cotton and rayon. Production is now a highly organized industry, with the men involved in the dyeing process, both men and women tying off the resists, and the women weaving the finished cloth on semi-automated frame looms.

The weft threads must be wound on to a simple rectangular frame that is approximately the same width as the finished cloth. This can be done by hand, but is now most usually achieved by drawing off threads from a rack containing twenty to thirty bobbins and wrapping them around a revolving frame.

Threads that are to be given identical motifs are bunched together on the tying frame, and the resist patterns are then tied in using plastic thread. To obtain modern

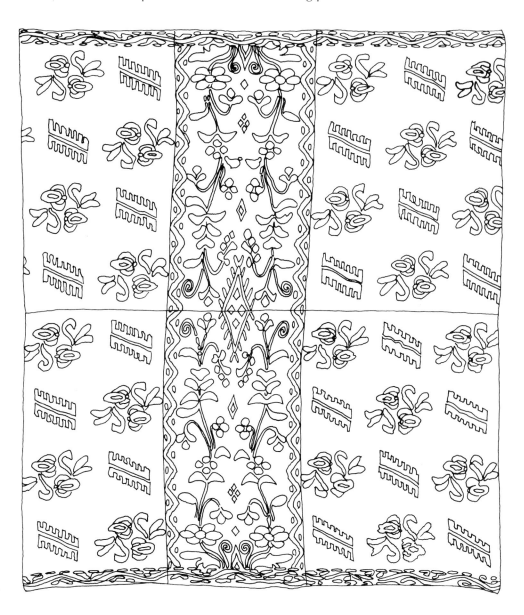

Weft-ikat sarong from Gresik, north-east Java, with floral motifs on the *kepala* and *badan*.

multicoloured weft-ikat cloth, a method is used known as *cetak*, a reversal of the traditional procedure. To dye a small area using the *cetak* technique, the motif is tied out in outline, and chemical dye spooned on. Once this has dried, the newly coloured area is tied up, and when other similar areas have been treated in the same manner with dye of the required colour, the whole frame can be dip-dyed to give the background colour. This method is more economical than the traditional method both in terms of time and materials.

Regional Styles

Palembang and Bangka   Beautiful weft-ikat silk *selendangs* known as *kain limar* were woven in Palembang, on Bangka Island and in the Riau archipelago. Often combined with *songket* borders or other elements scattered within the field, they were woven on backstrap looms. Those woven at Mentok, a small Chinese town on the west coast of Bangka, were patterned in blue and yellow on a red background, those of Palembang were in muted greens, yellows and blues on dark red. Both motifs and layout of *kain limar* have been influenced by *patola* textiles and are largely variations on floral and paisley patterns, geometric stars and circles, but they also include such typical Javanese designs as Garuda's wing motifs – the *lar* design depicting a wing, the *sawat* both wings and the tail. Narrow rows of birds, winged lions and *naga* dragons decorate the borders. Special weft-ikat silk and *songket selendangs* are worn by boys at their circumcision, and weft-ikat textiles have an important place in the series of gift exchanges so important to Sumatran culture.

Weft ikat is still woven on both backstrap looms and modern semi-automized looms in a few villages around Palembang. The designs are much simpler than of old, and the chemically derived colours rather garish. The Bugis community in Palembang continued to weave weft-ikat sarongs and yardage in their traditional Sulawesi style. Up till the beginning of this century silk weft ikat in fine diamond patterns used for *selendangs* was made around Solok in west Sumatra.

Bali   *Endek*, the Balinese name for silk weft ikat, was once the prerogative of noble families but now forms part of popular dress. *Endek* was originally a sumptuous silk fabric worn on ceremonial occasions as breastcloths and waistcloths, frequently combined with *songket* decoration.

Patterning on *endek* produced at the main weaving centre of Singaraja in Buleleng principality, north Bali, was based on variants of *patola* designs, and much of it took the form of the ritual *cepuk* cloth later to be produced on the island of Nusa Penida. There are also figurative representations, particularly of *wayang* puppets and the witches and demons of Balinese mythology. *Endek* textiles were also woven at Klungkung and Karangasem in the early part of this century.

In the 1930s *endek* production began to lose its exclusive association with the courts. On Nusa Penida and in the Tabanan area, much simpler *endek* cloth was woven on backstrap looms using hand-spun cotton or factory-spun and patterned yarn. New floral and geometric designs were introduced and found a ready popular market. From these origins grew the large commercial workshops (the first was started in Gianyar in the 1950s) with the emphasis now on the production of yardage rather than of individual cloths. Today, there are workshops all over Bali – at Gianyar, around Singaraja, at Sidemen, Jembrana and around Klungkung – producing weft-ikat fabric in cotton, synthetics and silk, which are aimed at the domestic, tourist and export markets.

With the transition to large factory production have come inevitable changes. Semi-mechanized fly-shuttle looms have replaced backstrap looms, and chemical dyes are now used. Flat plastic twine or strips of rubber now replace banana fibres to tie the resist. The *cetak* method is practised (known in Bali as *nyatri*), which entails spooning on synthetic dyes to the areas to be patterned, tying them off and then dipping them in a single dye bath to obtain the background colour.

The island of Nusa Penida was formerly used as a penitentiary by the kingdom of Klungkung and its dry climate is ideal for growing cotton. Here the weft-ikat cotton *cepuk* textiles are woven that have a ritual use all over Bali. *Cepuk* cloths always have a red background and weft-ikat patterning set within a rectangular grid. Down its side borders runs the white arrowhead pattern known as *gigi barong* (teeth of the protective Barong spirit).

Lombok   Western Lombok was for long periods dominated by the neighbouring Balinese kingdom of Klungkung across the water. Contemporary weft ikat produced in the semi-mechanized factories of Cakranegara and Sukarara is virtually indistinguishable from that of Bali. As in Bali, production is mainly yardage decorated using the *cetak* method.

Java   The weft-ikat industry in Java is now concentrated on the old port of Gresik, just north of Surabaya. With a strong Islamic tradition and a past history as a major centre for the import of Gujarati *patola*, weft-ikat production is in the hands of the town's large Arab community. Weaving is organized on a factory basis with men involved in the dyeing and resist binding and women operating the semi-automized looms. Colouring is achieved by the fast commercial *cetak* process using synthetic dyes. Production mainly comprises sarong lengths or yardage, with the typical Gresik cotton sarong featuring floral motifs on the *badan* and geometric motifs on the *kepala*. Colouring is in rather earthy, muted shades of greens, mustard yellow, rust and maroon. Much of the production is intended for export to neighbouring countries, but Gresik sarongs can be found for sale as far away as the Yemen and the Swahili coast of east Africa.

Troso, near Jepara on the north coast, is a very important centre for the production of weft ikat. Troso has no distinct style of its own, but produces weft ikat that is virtually indistinguishable from on the one hand that of Gresik and on the other the Bugis ikat of south Sulawesi.

The Bugis and Makassarese

The people inhabiting Makassar (now Ujung Pandang) and their neighbours, the Bugis, on the coast of south Sulawesi, were converted to Islam in the sixteenth century. They made a name for themselves as fierce defenders of the faith, intrepid seamen and traders, reaching the Gulf of Carpentaria in Australia well before the Europeans, and as fearsome pirates.

The Bugis in particular are famed for their weaving of silk sarongs with a weft-ikat pattern of iridiscent effect and usually plaid patterning. The *kepala* of the sarong is often decorated with layers of zig-zag waves in different colours. The Bugis have a penchant for bright blues, magentas, greens, purples and yellow. The weaving industry is centred on Sempange, Sengkang district, central-south Sulawesi. Silk thread comes from the nearby village of Tajuncu where a sericulture cottage industry has been set up with Japanese assistance, though much of the silk yarn used in the weaving industry is still imported. Sericulture is also practised in Soppeng. The ikat technique practised in Sengkang district is virtually identical with that of Gresik and Bali but Sulawesi ikat is valued for the number of colours (up to five) used in the cloth, and prized by Muslims in other parts of Indonesia who use it as clothing when making the Haj pilgrimage to Mecca. Bugis weavers in coastal Donggala add some warp-ikat patterning to the weft ikat. Colonies of Bugis are to be found in many coastal ports of the archipelago and the Bugis of Palembang, south Sumatra and of Samarinda, east Kalimantan, are noted for their fine weaving.

Geringsing – the fabled double-ikat cloths of Bali

Double-ikatting is a highly complex, time-consuming and laborious task only performed in three areas of the world: India, the home of the *patola*, Japan and the formerly remote village of Tenganan Pegeringsingan in north-east Bali. It entails resist dyeing both the warp and weft threads and then combining them to form the required design in plainweave.

Tenganan village is inhabited by a group of people known as the Bali Aga. They are worshippers of Indra and they and the other Balinese consider that they are a people apart. A noted expert on Balinese culture, Urs Ramseyer, conjectures that they may have been Vedic immigrants from ancient India, possibly bringing the art of double ikat with them from the eastern coast, perhaps from Orissa or Andhra Pradesh. The technique may have developed independently in Tenganan, however, or perhaps been deciphered from fragments of the type of coarsely woven *patola* exported to Indonesia.

Geringsing is woven on narrow backstrap looms. Two or more pieces can be sewn up to form skirtcloths, or else it can be used singly as a scarf. The Bali Aga are preoccupied with the concept of purity and the weaving of *geringsing* is seen as a social emblem which confirms their membership of the village. *Kamben geringsing* scarves are worn at times of the rites of passage of kinsmen and of village celebration, particularly during the festival of the fifth month, when young maidens swing on wooden swings. Different designs are worn by different groups in the village, such as youths and unmarried girls, and during these periods, girls of wealthy families will appear in public with an heirloom textile decorated in one of the prestigious *wayang* (shadow puppet) patterns. There used to be many taboos associated with the weaving of *geringsing*. Now the main prohibition is that women who are menstruating are excluded from the work. In the case of *geringsing wayang* a purification ceremony is conducted after the first ikat binding, consisting of flowers, *sirih* (betel) and old Chinese coins, and the resist tying can only be done by an old woman beyond child-bearing age. *Kamben geringsing* that are considered of inferior make by the Bali Aga are sold outside the village but are still used and valued all over Bali at rites of passage. As a cloth *geringsing* is considered to have magical protective properties; it is used, for instance, to cover a pillow on which the head of a person having their eye teeth filed will rest. It may also be laid over a corpse.

Rumours abound in Bali about the Bali Aga of Tenganan. One such is that the deep rust colour of *kamben geringsing* is derived from dried human blood. Though the dyeing process is long and painstaking, the dyestuffs used are wholly vegetable in origin. The *geringsing* are made of hand-spun cotton. Before dyeing the threads are pretreated with an overnight soak in a bath made of *kemiri* (candle-nut) oil and a wood-ash and water lye. They are then hung up to dry in the sun. The mordanting process is repeated for anything up to twelve days and will enhance the penetration of the red dye into the threads when the time comes for *mengkudu* dyeing.

The warp and the weft threads are then wound round their different dyeing frames. Since most *kamben geringsing* are quite small, the tying of the warp or weft resists for several cloths can be combined on a single frame. The threads for the individual cloths are separated after all the dyeing and ikat processes are finished. To aid the laying out of the weft threads a bobbin rack is used. Enough thread is wound around each bobbin to complete one whole motif on the woven cloth. Threads are then drawn off the bobbins and wrapped around the dyeing frame. The pattern is then bound in, and after the dyeing process is complete the individual threads are returned to their bobbins. To obtain a matching, integrated design with the double-ikat process, the spacing of both warp and weft ties must be most accurately measured. Guidelines are drawn in charcoal perpendicular to the threads as a measuring aid.

An old weaving is used as a model when tying the pattern. There are approximately twenty basic designs in *geringsing*, which are mainly floral and geometric. The most spectacular and most revered, however, are the *wayang kebo* or *wayang putri*, which

Kamben geringsing from Tenganan Pegeringsingan, Bali.

feature *wayang* puppet figures in light brown on a purplish black background, grouped around a star-shaped temple motif. They are thought to have been made originally for the courts of Bali and east Java.

The bound warp and weft threads are sent out of the village to be dyed indigo blue. They are then put back on their binding frames so that some of their ties may be undone to let in the *mengkudu* red dye. The indigo coloured areas are always overdyed in red, resulting in the characteristic dark, rust-brown colour of *kamben geringsing*. The warp is then laid out on the simple backstrap loom and the cloth is woven in a loose, plain balanced weave, using a pick to readjust the weft thread with every pass of the shuttle to make sure it is in correct alignment with the warp threads.

Plangi and Tritik

The tie-and-dye cloths of Bali were made in shades of yellow, orange, purple and green, the colours of the rainbow. The Indonesian word for 'rainbow' is *plangi* and it is by this term that tie-and-dye cloths are known all over the archipelago. With the tie-and-dye technique small areas of the cloth are pinched up and bound round tightly with thread to form a resist. After the required areas have been tied, the cloth is dip-dyed and upon untying a pattern of circles is revealed, in the original ground colour of the cloth against

Selendang from Palembang, Sumatra, decorated with the plangi and tritik techniques on imported Shantung silk.

the newly dyed background colour. The technique may be varied by inserting tiny stones into the tied-up portions of the cloth, to pad them out and give them shape. The plangi cloths may be dyed in a series of colours, always starting with the lighter colours and ending up with the darkest, with different areas being tied and untied at each of the dyeing stages to form a complex multicoloured pattern. Large portions of a cloth to be dyed are often bound up in a banana leaf so that different sections of the cloth end up with contrasting background colours.

Plangi cloths are made in Bali, Lombok, Java, coastal Kalimantan, Sulawesi and most notably in Palembang, south-east Sumatra, where the Indian derivation of this technique is most obviously shown. (Tie-and-dye *bandhani* shawls are still made in Jamnagar, Gujarat, for the Indonesian market.)

In Indonesia the plangi technique is usually combined with another resist-dyeing method known as tritik. With tritik the resist is stitched into the cloth, usually with strong pineapple thread that will not break when, after every few inches, the thread is pulled tightly to gather the cloth. Tritik patterns are linear; the cloth is compressed along the line of stitching thus forming a resist and preventing the dye from seeping in.

Central Java once had a fine plangi and particularly tritik tradition whereby, often in combination with batik, fine *selendang*, *dodot* and other cloths were produced. Now production is confined to very simple headcloths and *kemben* breastcloths in cotton, usually in one background colour only, though spots of different colour can be painted in after dyeing has been completed. Here the technique is known by the Javanese term *jumpatan*. Gresik is also a plangi and tritik centre. Balinese plangi cloths are hung at tooth-filing ceremonies, but much plangi made in Bali today is crude in colour and design and aimed at the tourist. In the Rongkong district of the Toraja-lands of Sulawesi, long cotton banners were made to hang on poles before the houses of the dead. They were simply but most effectively decorated in the plangi technique with circular motifs said to represent the sun and stars.

Palembang is the only centre today producing truly interesting plangi and tritik. Complex Indian-influenced patterns are worked on cotton, silk and artificial silk and afterwards embellished in *prada* goldwork to produce stunning (but expensive) *kain* and *selendang*. Palembang was famous for its pre-World War II manufacture of plangi and tritik *selendangs* worked on flimsy imported Chinese silk, either in extremely simple geometric patterns, or intricate layouts featuring the Kashmiri *butta* cone design.

74 (Opposite) Detail of contemporary weft-ikat yardage from Gianyar, Bali. Dyed using the *cetak* process.

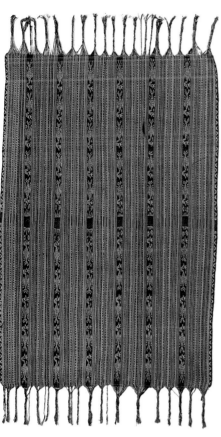

75 (Opposite) *Beti futus* warp-ikat *selendang* from central Timor. Motifs of men and of crocodiles eating fish adorn the field.

76, 77 (Above and right) *Futus manu ana* man's warp-ikat cotton waistcloth from Isana, Timor, featuring cockerels – the symbol of bravery.

78 *Selendang* of warp-ikat cotton from Niki-Niki, west Timor, with a central design of anthropomorphic figures.

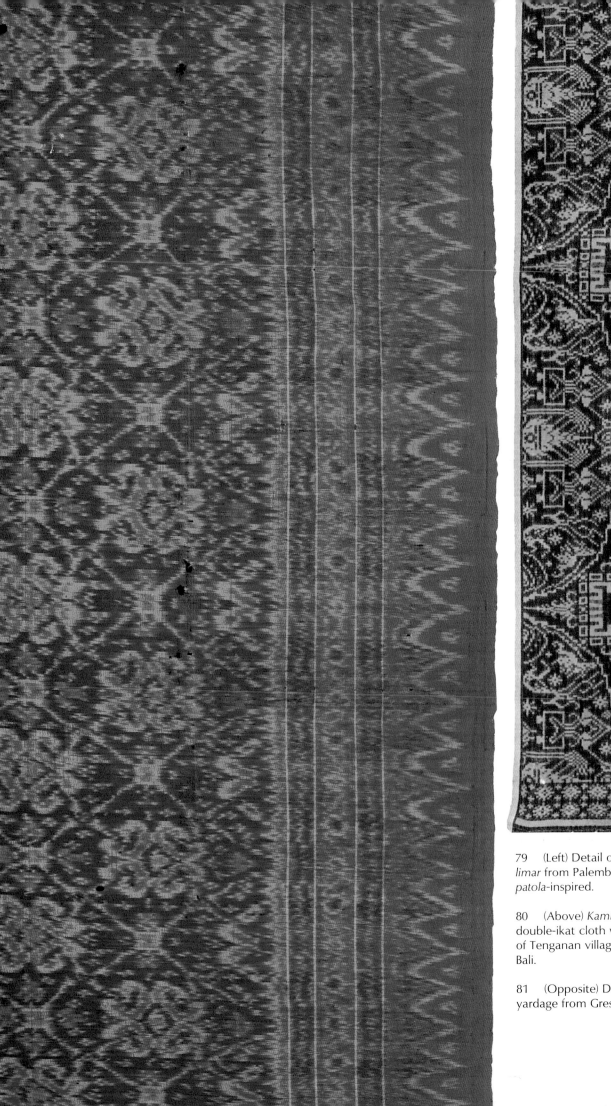

79   (Left) Detail of a weft-ikat silk *kain limar* from Palembang. The patterns are *patola*-inspired.

80   (Above) *Kamben geringsing*, a ritual double-ikat cloth woven by the Bali Aga of Tenganan village and revered all over Bali.

81   (Opposite) Detail of weft-ikat yardage from Gresik, east Java.

82 *Seko mandi* warp-ikat funeral shroud. Made of cotton, by the Toraja of Sulawesi.

83 *Seko mandi* made for the tourist market, featuring sacrificial buffalo. Probably from Mamuja, Sulawesi.

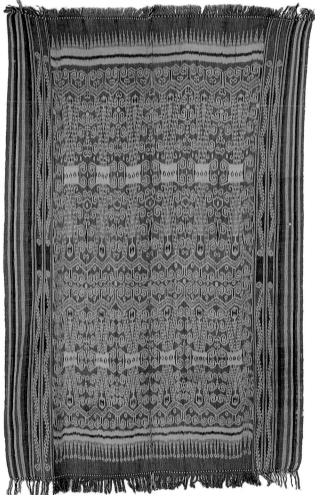

84 *Pua kumbu* cotton warp-ikat ritual cloth, woven by Iban tribeswomen from Sarawak.

85 (Opposite) Iban *pua kumbu* hanging from Sarawak, woven in warp-ikat cotton for fertility rituals, with consecutive rows of male and female figures.

86　(Opposite) Warp-ikat *selendang* from Beboki, Timor.

87　Sarong with *patola*-inspired designs in warp-ikat cotton from Lio district, Flores.

88   Silk *selendang* with plangi and tritik designs from
Palembang, Sumatra.

89   Plangi and tritik, Indian-influenced motifs and Kashmiri
butta cones, worked on thin Chinese silk in Palembang.

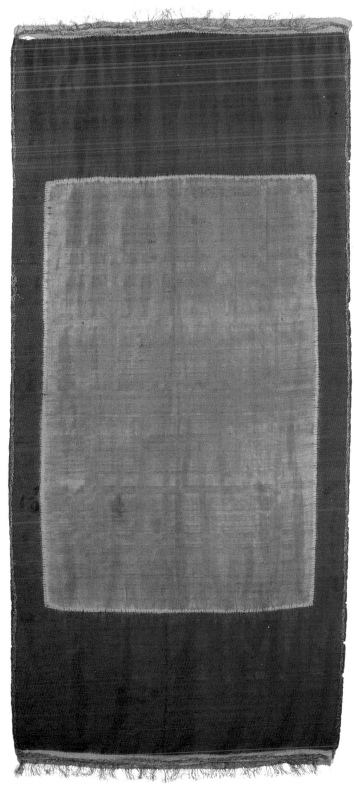

90   Plangi and tritik silk shawl, Palembang.

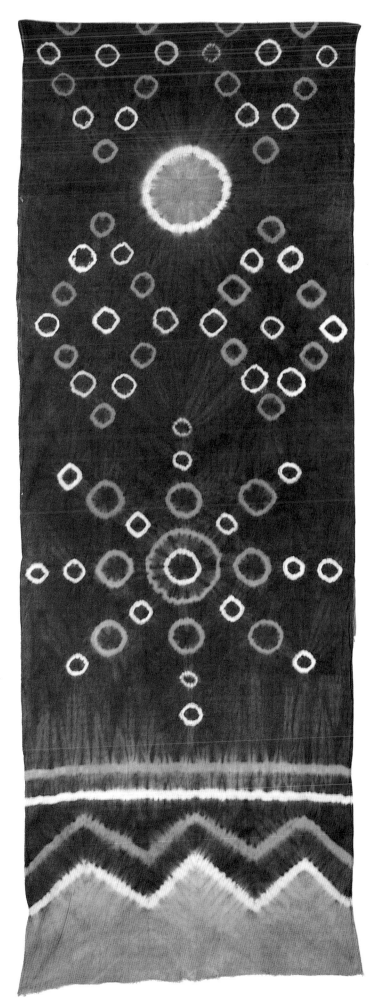

91   *Roto* festival banner decorated in the plangi technique by the Toraja of Rongkong, Sulawesi.

92   Warp-ikat sarong from Savu, decorated with floral bands and cupids.

93   (Opposite, above) Man wearing a Savunese *selendang*, selling palm wine from *lontar* palm-leaf containers. Waingapu, Sumba.

94   Warp-ikat sarong of hand-spun cotton, from Savu.

95, 96   Warp-ikat cotton *hinggi*
hipcloths from east Sumba. The above
example is decorated with motifs of
Komodo monitor lizards and skeletons
with a *patola ratu* central band. The
unusual *hinggi* (right) is dyed in two
different background colours. One end is
decorated in warp-ikat with Chinese
dragons, the other with the Dutch coat
of arms.

97, 98   Warp-ikat cotton *hinggis* from Prailiu, east Sumba. The cloth (above) depicts peacocks, civet cats, monkeys and winged celestial beings. The *hinggi* at right shows a mounted raja surrounded by attendants.

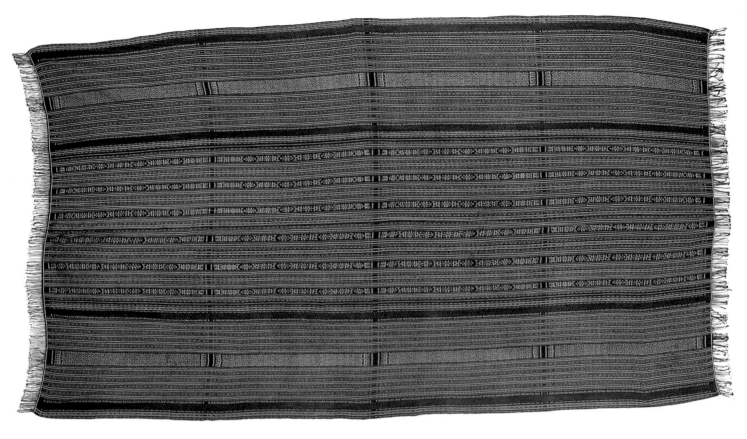

99 Warp-ikat *selimut* from Beboki, Timor.

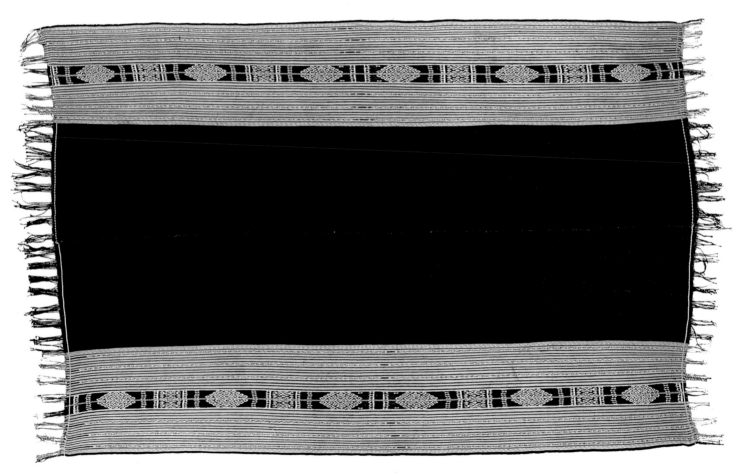

100 *Selimut* with a plain indigo central field and warp-ikat borders, made in Molo, west Timor.

101 (Opposite) Chemically dyed warp-ikat cotton *selendang*, from Maliana, east Timor.

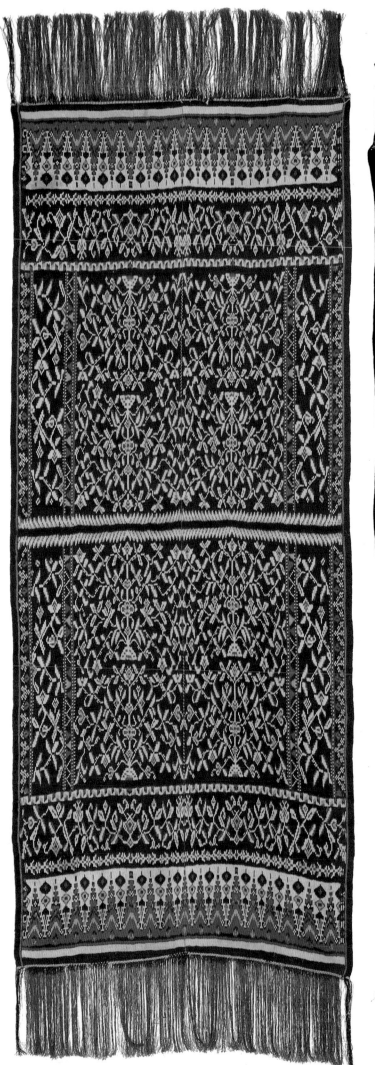

Opposite
102, 103 Warp-ikat cotton *selendangs* from Rote, patterned with European-style floral designs.

104, 105 Cotton warp-ikat *selendangs* made in Savu (above) by the 'Greater Blossom' clan, and in Rote (right).

106 (Left) Cotton warp-ikat sarong with *patola*-inspired designs, from Nggela, Flores.

107 Warp-ikat cotton sarong woven at Ndona, near Ende, Flores.

108 (Opposite) Warp-ikat sarong from Wolonjita, Flores, with indigo-dyed *patola* motifs in lateral stripes.

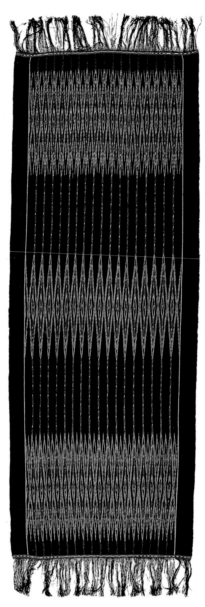

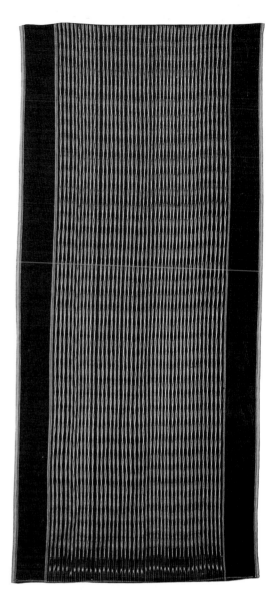

109   Warp-ikat ritual *ulos* cloth made by the Toba Batak of Sumatra.

110   Toba Batak *ulos sibolang* decorated with three bands of warp-ikat patterning against a blue background. This textile is worn as a headdress by a widow.

111   Toba Batak *ulos mangiring,* used as a baby sling and patterned with warp-ikat arrowhead motifs.

112   Warp-ikat cotton *selendang* of the 'Lesser Blossom' clan of Savu.

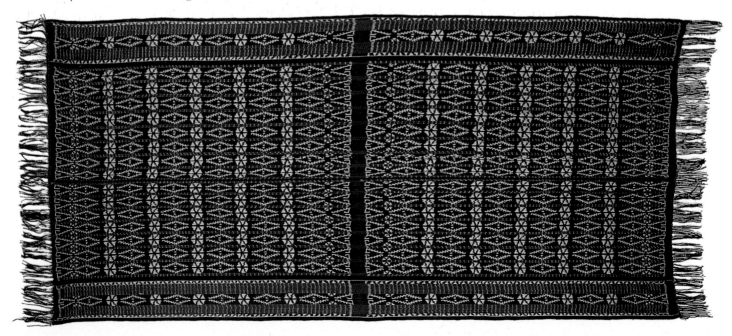

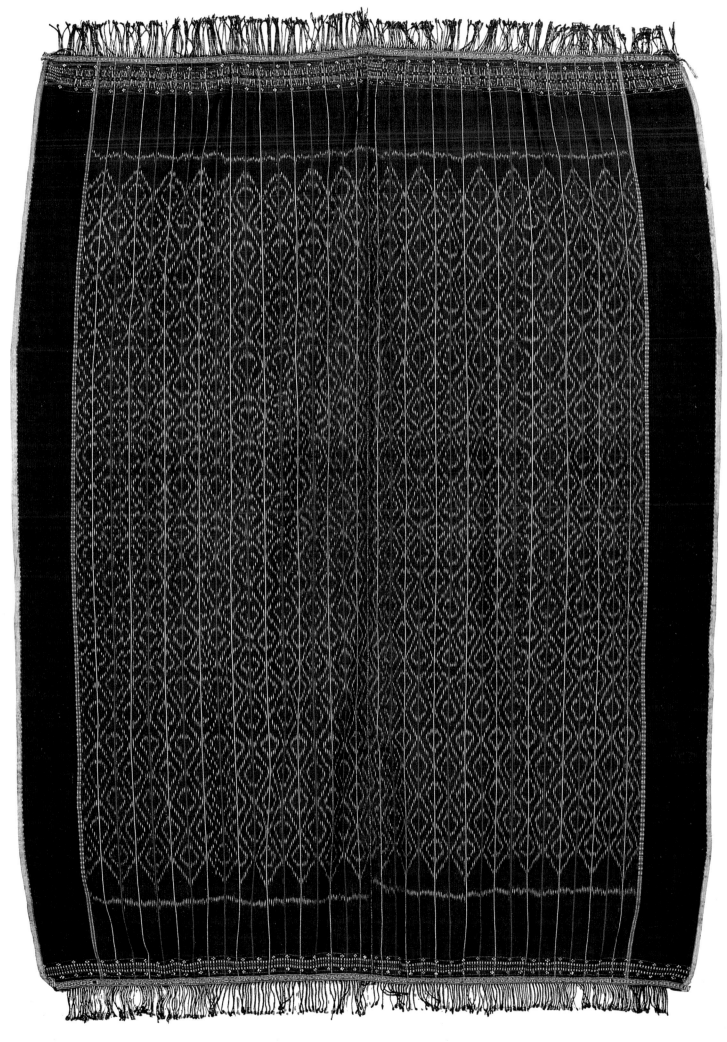

113   *Ulos* woven in the Porsea area of north Sumatra by the Toba Batak for the Angkola Batak. Beads are incorporated at the top and bottom, just above the twined borders.

114   Supplementary-warp decorated border of a *lau pahudu* woman's sarong from east Sumba. Patterns are of Chinese dragons and other animals. The yellow and blue details are painted in after the weaving is completed.

5   The Art of Embellishment

Indonesians have a love for lavishly embellished textiles – inlaid with additional wefts or warps of gold or silver, silk or cotton thread, or decorated with embroidery, appliqué or shellwork. The most widespread of these decorative techniques is the craft of *songket* brocade weaving. *Songket* cloth is woven in those regions of the archipelago most affected by Malay or Bugis immigration – that is, coastal eastern Sumatra, the Riau archipelago, Kalimantan, Sulawesi and Sumbawa. It is also woven in such non-Muslim areas as Bali and some parts of Lombok, and by Iban tribeswomen in Sarawak, north Borneo.

Supplementary Weft

Songket weaving involves the use of extra-weft threads of gold, silver or silken material, and is one version of a more generalized technique known as supplementary-weft weaving. With this technique, supplementary threads are inserted into the same shed as the ordinary wefts and are floated over certain selected warp threads to form distinctive patterns of a colour and texture that contrasts with the ground cloth. The supplementary-weft threads can either be worked continuously or, when only small areas of extra-weft patterning are required, extra-weft threads may be just worked back and forth across the selected warp threads only and not taken across the full width of the cloth. This is known as discontinuous supplementary-weft weaving.

   Songket weaving is an extremely complex process. Before any weaving can commence the different combinations of warp threads to be raised to form the various pattern sheds must be worked out. Firstly the warp threads are set out, counted and the various threads to be raised marked out at particular places to form the extra-weft pattern. Sumatra, with its rich and varied textile tradition, has two main centres of *songket* production, the prolific city of Palembang, and Pandai Sikat near Bukittinggi. Palembang *songket* is woven on strongly built backstrap looms and utilizes a cotton warp to provide a firm ground for the golden extra-weft thread which is set against a silk weft background. The most common method used to form the extra-weft pattern at Palembang involves the setting up of a series of secondary heddle rods, which lie behind the main heddles. The warp threads that will form the pattern are lifted and sticks inserted whilst leashes are tied around the threads and then attached to rods. The sticks are then removed. The apparatus for this method of *songket* weaving is very time-consuming to set up but very flexible in operation as the string pattern heddle rods can be lifted in any order to insert *lidi* pattern sticks for a particular pattern.

   Palembang *songket* has a large repertoire of floral motifs that combine with end-patterns of *tumpal* (triangular spear shapes), or the *pucuk rebung* bamboo-shoot motif. The silk yarn used is imported from Singapore and the gold thread from India, but if a very prestigious *kain songket* is to be woven, real gold thread is taken from a discarded old textile. Palembang before World War II produced fabulous *songket* cloth using high-quality fourteen-carat gold thread.

   Minangkabau *songket* from Pandai Sikat is woven on Malay shaft looms with metallic yarn from Singapore. Pandai Sikat *songket* is often very densely patterned, so much so

A border of embroidered figures of monitor lizards, from Ayotupas, west Timor.

that often the base cloth is not visible. *Songket* is worn for ceremonial and festive wear and Minangkabau women's *songket selendangs* are folded into the horned headdresses traditional to the area. Common designs are of flowers and leaves depicted in angular star-shaped form with *tumpal* or *pucuk rebung* end pieces. Other centres for Minangkabau *songket* are Silungkang, forty-five miles from Bukittinggi, which produces coarse work on cotton, and the villages around Paya Kumbuh, where *songket* is woven to both traditional and modern designs.

Minangkabau women wearing ceremonial dress, west Sumatra.

Regional Styles

Bali   Like Sumatra, Bali has a long and varied tradition of weaving *kain songket*. With the Balinese love for ceremony, festival and drama, splendid *songket* textiles have always been in great demand. Weaving of *kain songket* was originally the preserve of aristocratic women and the wearing of them restricted to the upper castes, but with the liberalization of Balinese society during the last fifteen years, *kain songket* is worn as festive garb by all strata of society. Balinese *songket* was traditionally woven in silk for the aristocratic market and on a harder-wearing cotton background for those intended for dance or theatrical performances. Because of the high cost of silk, over the last thirty years rayon and artificial silk have been used for the base cloth, and real or artificial silk in different colours for the supplementary weft threads as an alternative to the more expensive golden and silver metallic threads. Balinese *kain songket* are woven on the onomatopoeically named *cag-cag* backstrap looms. Before weaving commences the warp threads must be carefully laid out and each one drawn individually through a reed. As in Palembang, only cloth of a limited width can be produced. Wider cloths have to be made up of two narrow *kain songket* joined together. Supplementary weft threads are wound on small pieces of cardboard and after three passes of supplementary weft threads they are bound in by three picks of the ground weft. Patterns are taken from old cloths or a woven sample, or alternatively a pattern model may be made up out of sticks and yarn.

Sidemen, a village between Klungkung and Karangasem in east Bali, is famed for its fine *kain songket*, as is Tabanan in central Bali and the Singaraja area to the north.

Lombok   *Kain songket* with patterning very similar to that of neighbouring east Bali is woven by Sasak weavers on body-tension looms at Sukarara. Motifs are floral and geometric, of rosettes, zig-zags and triangles.

Sumbawa   Lying close to Sulawesi, the island of Sumbawa was partially conquered by the Buginese, who brought with them an austere form of Islam, and in its wake various weaving skills, of which *songket* was the most important. *Kain songket* in Sumbawa is woven using a rather soft gimp metallic thread and the sarongs feature a *kepala* with facing rows of *tumpal* between which are set figures of men in boats, often surrounded by fish and birds. *Songket* is woven on backstrap looms in Sumbawa using pattern heddle rods. The looms used in the courts are beautiful artifacts made of heavy carved and gilded wood.

Ship Cloths of Lampung

The Paminggir and other neighbouring groups of Lampung in south-west Sumatra wove extremely intricate ceremonial cloths in the extra-weft technique. The cloths were woven in three basic shapes: the *palepai*, a long, narrow textile, often more than three yards long, the *tatibin*, another narrow cloth, about a yard long, and the *tampan*, varying in dimension from about 15 cm (6 in) to over 90 cm (3 ft) square.

The most spectacular motif worked, particularly on the *palepai*, is that of a ship with a great curving prow and stern, crammed with human figures and with a mast which often branches out into a tree of life. The idea of a ship of the dead, carrying souls away to the after-life, was once common throughout Indonesia, South-East Asia and the Pacific islands. Indeed, wood-carved ships of the dead were a central theme in the art of the Batak of Sumatra and certain Dyak groups in Kalimantan.

Palepai were only ever made in the Kroe region around Lake Ranau. The use of both *palepai* and *tatibin* were restricted to clan leaders and other social superiors. *Tampan* on the other hand had a much wider geographical distribution in Lampung and could be made and worn by any social stratum. The motifs worked on *tampan* were much more varied than those on *palepai* and *tatibin*. Large figures of birds and trees or repetitive arrangements of human figures were depicted, as well as ships with animals and people on deck, set against a sea and sky crammed with marine and bird life. For centuries Lampung was an important centre for international trade in pepper. The wealth generated therefrom was ostentatiously spent on great ceremonies marking rites of passage, at which the display of intricately woven *tampan* and *palepai* would have formed an integral part. Similar cloths are made by the Buddhist Tai peoples of north Thailand, Laos, and Xishuang Banna, south-west China. So perhaps the extra-weft cloths of both Lampung and these Tai areas share a Buddhist ancestry as well as Dong-Son influence on their motifs.

The production of *palepai*, *tatibin* and *tampan* ceased around the turn of the century. This was due to a number of factors, a loss of prosperity which followed a decline in the pepper trade, the lack of a skilled weaving force resulting from the abolition of slavery in the mid-nineteenth century, and a concurrent change in marriage traditions. These cloths were woven on backstrap body-tension looms and patterned by coloured supplementary wefts, usually in cotton (rarely silk), on a background of unbleached cotton in plainweave. Though none of the looms has survived, the textile scholar Gittinger concludes that they were discontinuously warped looms fitted with a reed.

Ship cloths are now much treasured outside Lampung, and have been collected by foreigners since the 1930s – original pieces are now very rare. In 1975 Haji Abdul Kadir, a weaver of Pekalongan, north Java, was challenged to make a copy of an old *palepai* ship cloth. He succeeded so well, using techniques akin to those of Lampung, that many such imitation ship cloths have since been produced. The vast majority of ship cloths for sale in the tourist markets of Jakarta and Bali are of this origin. Using the same supplementary technique Sasak weavers in Lombok wove a square textile similar to the *tampan* which is known as an *usap*. *Usap* featured either geometric designs or motifs of mythical beasts.

Extra-weft Sarongs of Flores

The Manggarai region of western Flores was for part of the seventeenth century ruled from Bima in east Sumbawa. The influence of this period is reflected in the distinctive extra-weft weaving which decorates Manggarai sarongs. The sarongs of a deep indigo blue are woven on a body-tension loom with a discontinuous warp and are worked with geometrical motifs in many colours with the supplementary-weft technique. The supplementary weft-work is concentrated on the *kepala* with other decorative elements scattered over the field of the sarong. The best Manggarai cloths have a row of *tumpal* along each selvedge, worked in the tapestry technique to interlock with the adjoining weft.

Pilih

An unusual adaptation of the supplementary weft technique called *pilih* is practised by the versatile Iban weavers of Sarawak. The *pilih* method is used mainly to decorate Kalambi jackets and waistcoats for men and boys and the men's shouldercloths known as *dandong*. With this technique the supplementary threads, which are carried by small shuttles across the weft and float on the surface of the woven cloth, form only the background of the desired pattern. The main design motifs are created by the background weft, which appears on the surface when the supplementary weft is taken to the underside of the cloth. *Pilih* cloth is woven by the Iban in stripes that alternate in colour (usually red and black).

Sungkit

The term *sungkit* is derived from the Malay word for 'needle'. The *sungkit* method of decorating textiles with discontinuous supplementary weft threads may best be described as 'embroidery on the loom'. The technique is used by the Iban or Sarawak to decorate ritual *pua* cloths, *kalambi* jackets and *sirat* loincloths, particularly those of *manang* shamen. The Atoni and Belu people of Timor used *sungkit* extensively to decorate their sarongs, *selendangs*, purses and *sirih* bags. In Timor the technique is known as *sotis*, or *pauf*.

With *sungkit*, the motifs are worked using small bobbins, or bone or porcupine-quill needles, to wrap different-coloured threads two or three times around appropriate warp threads. After each row of the supplementary *sungkit* pattern has been completed, one or two picks of the ground weft are passed across to secure the *sungkit* threads. Because of the time-consuming nature of this method, it is usually only used to decorate narrow widths of cloth. Pattern designs worked in *sungkit* appear as precisely the same on both faces of the cloth. Small details of the *sungkit* design may be embroidered after the weaving process has finished. It is very often difficult to distinguish between *sungkit* and embroidery on a completed cloth. In an embroidered cloth, the supplementary threads will have penetrated some of the ground threads.

Tapestry and Tablet Weaving

Tapestry weaving, which produces mosaic designs with differently coloured discontinuous weft threads, is found in a few of the outlying islands and also sometimes in Sumba and the Batak area of Sumatra. It is used to decorate the borders of some Iban warriors' *kalambi* jackets and to create sashes and headbands for Atoni head-hunters from Timor. Tablet weaving is a technique practised in south Sulawesi to make ceremonial belts with magical inscriptions in Arabic script. It is also found in Java. The warp yarns are threaded through small square tablets usually of bone or tortoise-shell. These tablets are rotated to form the sheds and the resulting textile will be a narrow warp-faced band.

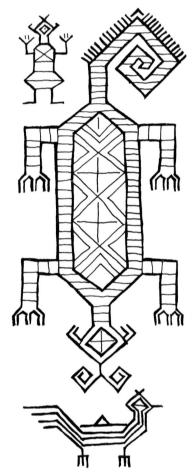

Sungkit weft-wrapped depictions of a monitor lizard, a bird and a female figure, from a woman's sarong, Ayotupas, west Timor.

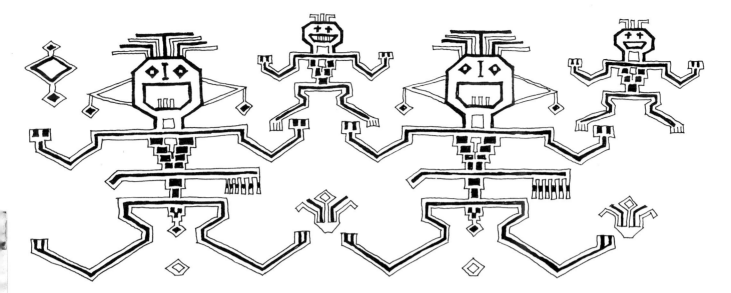

A *sungkit* border of head-hunters and women from an Iban shaman's jacket, Sarawak.

Supplementary Warp

The ancient art of supplementary warp weaving is practised in the Nusa Tenggara group of islands, in Bali, Timor and most famously in Sumba. This method of weaving is also used to decorate textiles in Ternate and Tidore in the Moluccas.

In the royal villages of Pau and Rende in east Sumba, noblewomen weave a woman's sarong known as *lau pahudu*. This sarong is worn at funeral and other rites by women of the aristocracy. The main body of the sarong is patterned with plain lateral stripes or occasionally with warp ikat. The most striking area of design, though, is in the lower border, which has motifs of standing or dancing men, Chinese dragons, skull trees, birds or animals worked in a supplementary warp of heavy, light-coloured yarn against a dark background weave. Long sashes are also woven in the same technique with repetitive motifs of human figures and animals. The tourist demand for these pieces is now so high that, breaking with tradition, young men as well as women are now weaving them on traditional looms with very long warps.

Before any supplementary warp-patterned textiles are woven in east Sumba the pre-dyed ground-warp threads are laid out on a body-tension loom equipped with two heddles. This warp is circular and continuous. Likewise the supplementary warp threads which are thicker and lighter in colour, usually white, are laid over the ground-weft threads, also forming a continuous circular warp. The weaver then places a bamboo stick between the ground and extra warps, near the warp beam, to ensure that the two sets of warps do not become entangled. This also helps to maintain and control the tension in the warp threads and to ensure that they remain aligned.

A small pattern model made of string and sticks is used as a guide to setting out the extra-warp pattern. Many small wooden *lidi* splints are then set into place, picking up the appropriate supplementary-warp threads to form the pattern. Where they have been raised by the *lidi* sticks the supplementary-warp threads will appear on the surface of the finished cloth to form the pattern. When they do not appear on the surface the extra-warp threads will form a continuous float on the underside of the completed cloth.

To weave the supplementary warp-patterned cloth the weaver inserts a thicker stick alongside the desired *lidi* stick and lifts it along with one or other of the string heddle rods to form a shed into which is passed the bobbin with the weft thread. Thus the *lidi* sticks are lifted in sequence forming a supplementary pattern in twill weave.

The same technique was occasionally used in Bali to make the long banners known as *lamak* that are hung from altars or on long poles at many Balinese festivals. They were

Extra-warp decoration in the shape of a monitor lizard, from an east Sumban man's sash.

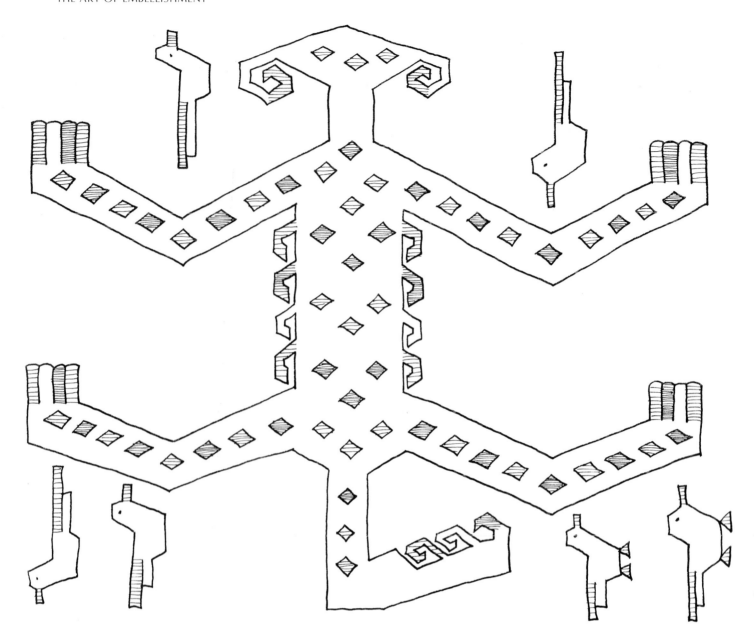

A cat-like figure and gulls worked in supplementary warp on a man's sash, from east Sumba.

woven with a rather loose white cotton supplementary warp against a darker cotton ground. The patterns were made up of diamond-shapes and usually featured *cili* figures – stylized depictions of the rice goddess Dewi Sri. Today *lamak* banners are almost always made out of plaited straw but occasionally they are made of cloth decorated with embroidery or appliqué. The supplementary warp technique is also employed in parts of Timor to work decorative borders to men's *selendang* shawls.

Embroidery, Appliqué, Beadwork and Shellwork

Embroidery in the Indonesian archipelago is mainly found in those coastal areas settled by Islamic Malay peoples, and apart from some mirrorwork in the Lampung area it mostly consists of couched metal-threadwork. The Malay courts of Sumatra and Kalimantan had longstanding marriage relations with both mainland Chinese and those settled in the Indonesian islands. Indonesian metal-thread embroidery is particularly associated with these courts and reflects Chinese cultural influence.

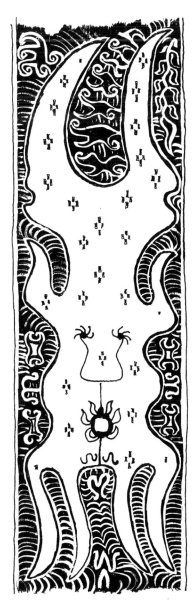

Detail of a sea creature, embroidered in satinstitch on a decorative band of a Paminggir woman's sarong, from the mountainous interior of Lampung, south Sumatra.

Splendid Chinese embroideries of couched gold thread on a bright silk background have for many centuries been hung in the homes, shrines and temples of the Chinese quarters of the towns of Indonesia. These embroideries, and to a lesser extent those from India, the Middle East and Turkey, had a profound effect on Indonesian styles of embroidery. Sumatra possesses the greatest abundance of embroidery and the widest range of styles.

In Aceh, which had close links with both the Mughal and Turkish empires, the Minangkabau area and Jambi and Palembang, there is a long tradition of couched metal-threadwork. Rectangular hangings and pennanted friezes (reminiscent of Gujarati *torans*) were produced, along with square covers, which were displayed at festivals. They took particular prominence at weddings, where the bridal bed, with its sumptuous decoration, provided a splendid backdrop for the bride and groom. Motifs are of flowers, foliage and birds, often embellished with mirrors or small fragments of mica. Amongst the Malay peoples of the coasts of Sumatra and Kalimantan, ceremonial bolster cushions for display on the bridal bed were decorated with end-panels of couched metal-threadwork, appliqué or even cross-stitch canvas work.

Gold thread embroidery often provided a substitute for the more expensive and time-consuming *songket* brocade, being used to embellish the cuffs of men's ceremonial trousers, for instance. Metallic-thread embroidery is worked on frames. In Aceh and western Sumatra patterns are often based on Turkish embroidery, which would have been imported to Aceh in the seventeenth and eighteenth centuries. Popular items are square food covers or cushion covers on which metallic thread is couched down with tiny stitches on a satin fabric.

In a less sophisticated and less court-orientated manner are embroidered the *tapis* sarongs of the Paminggir of the mountainous interior of Lampung, south Sumatra. Embroidered bands, usually in white, with designs of men, ships, snakes, many tentacled octopuses and mythical beasts, are worked in satin stitch and set against a sombre brown warp-ikat background.

The wealthier Paminggir people of the coast make *tapis* with designs of people, horses and riders couched in golden thread on a plainweave striped background. Women of the neighbouring Kauer people make extensive use of tiny mirrors called *cermuk*, which are combined with an embroidered scroll motif into bands around their *tapis* sarongs. This *tapis* is worn with a ceremonial jacket which has *cermuk* mirrorwork down the front lapels, many tiny cowrie shells applied around the collar and a woven *songket* backpiece bordered with shellwork. Flat metallic ribbon embroidery, probaby of Middle Eastern origin, is worked on gauze-like cloth in Aceh and Sumbawa to produce shoulder cloths and headcloths. Quite crude chainstitch work of human figures is practised in Sumba and wherever the *sungkit* weft-wrapping technique is found – in Timor and Sarawak, for instance – women are also skilled at embroidery. Appliqué in imported cloth, stitched to a plain contrasting ground, is practised by the Kenyah-Bahau Dyaks of Borneo.

All over the archipelago beads, seeds and shells which all have an intrinsic value have often been applied to cloth. In Lampung, beadwork was sometimes used as a substitute for weaving to make *tampan* and *palepai*. It was also once common on the textiles of the Toraja, the Bataks and the Dyaks, and was found in Sumba and Flores. Some beads are extremely valuable. In Borneo a single bead of a certain type could once have bought a slave or a whole village, thus both the value of the textile is increased and its protective qualities enhanced due to the 'hard' nature of this adornment with beads. Ritual sarongs of the Ngada people of west Flores are decorated with star and animal figures worked in beads. In Sumba split *nassa* shells are attached to important ritual sarongs known as *lau hada*. These shells are combined with beadwork to form sexually exaggerated male and female shapes with reptilian forms poised below their genitalia. The Taman of Kalimantan apply *nassa* shells to waistcoats and *bidang* skirts. Designs are of animals, lizards and dragons. Beads are worked with a needle by the Toraja in looped circular rows, to form conical *kandaure* covers which are used at festivals and canopy bodies at funerals. The Toraja also make beadwork belts which are worn by dancers of either sex. The southern Bataks wear interesting ceremonial beadwork belts worked with imported Venetian beads.

On the upper reaches of the Kapuas river in Kalimantan the Taman branch of the Maloh tribe make beautiful beadwork skirts and waistcoats out of imported glass beads, which they wear on ceremonial occasions. The Taman do not weave themselves, but will trade their beadwork for warp-ikat cloths from the neighbouring Iban. Lastly, in Irian Jaya, a region otherwise not noted for its textile skills, the women of the Cenderawasih area make beadwork dance aprons with motifs of reptiles and lozenges.

Painted Cloths

The Toraja of Sulawesi use sacred cotton cloths known as *ma'a* as funeral shrouds and as inaugural banners at the dedication of a new house. Older *ma'a* are printed or painted Indian trade cloths. For many years the Toraja have created their own indigenous *ma'a*, sometimes imitating Indian patterns but most often painting a central design of a buffalo being led into a corral surrounded by block-printed crosses that represent stars.

Bark Cloth

Bark cloth was once used all over the archipelago for everyday garments and for ritual and magical purposes. Indeed, the textile scholar Kooijman considers that Sulawesi was the centre from which bark cloth-making skills spread to the rest of the Indonesian–Polynesian world. There are remarkable similarities between the words for the implements used in its making and the actual cloth, between Sulawesi and the Polynesian islands of the Pacific.

The Toraja of Sulawesi once made extremely beautiful bark cloth headcloths and ponchos, which were brush-painted or stamped with star-shaped designs in as many as four colours. Although the Toraja still make bark cloth, which they know as *fuya*, they no longer decorate it, and it is looked down on as unsophisticated and a sign of poverty. The people of Palu district to the north of the Toraja lands still make and use bark cloth. The Murut tribe of Borneo make waistcoats and other garments out of bark cloth.

Bark cloth is a felted rather than a woven fabric and must be strengthened by lines of stitching or embroidery worked perpendicularly to the grain of the fabric. Bark cloth is made from the bark of a variety of trees, notably the paper mulberry tree and the breadfruit tree. The outer bark of saplings or branches is taken off, then the inner layer of bark is laid on a log and beaten with stone or wooden beaters with a cross-grooved surface. In the process the fibres spread out and are felted together to form cloth. Bark cloth called *deluwang* was once made in Java. The fact that this craft was confined to a specific caste of priests attests to its ancient origins. The arts of painting, embroidery, appliqué and particularly the adornment of cloth with shells and beads likewise must have roots that stretch way back into the past.

Supplementary-warp weavings are prized as heritage textiles on some of the Indonesian islands and such complex techniques as *sungkit* and *pilih* would appear to be of indigenous origin. Supplementary weft methods of weaving such as *songket* are practised mainly in those areas of the archipelago subject to Muslim influence, however, a likely indication that they are imported techniques. As such, they stand as yet another testimony to the Indonesian genius for adaptation. The islanders lavish painstaking care on the creation of their textiles and prize the resulting beautifully patterned fabrics as their forefathers in the spice islands did before them, literally at a value beyond gold itself.

115 (Opposite) Silk trouser cuffs from Palembang, decorated with couched metal-thread embroidery.

116 Ceremonial *lau hada* sarong from east Sumba, embellished with *nassa* shells worked into a pattern of a woman, lizard and attendant animals.

117 (Right) *Dandong* man's shouldercloth, with patterns of anthropomorphic lizards worked in the *pilih* technique by the Iban Dyaks of Sarawak.

118 Chainstitch-embroidered cloth, cotton on cotton, from east Sumba. The design is of a male figure, lizards and lions.

119 (Opposite) Embroidered sarong with motifs of women and Komodo lizards from Ayotupas, Timor.

120   The front and back of a Kauer woman's festival jacket, from Lampung, south Sumatra.

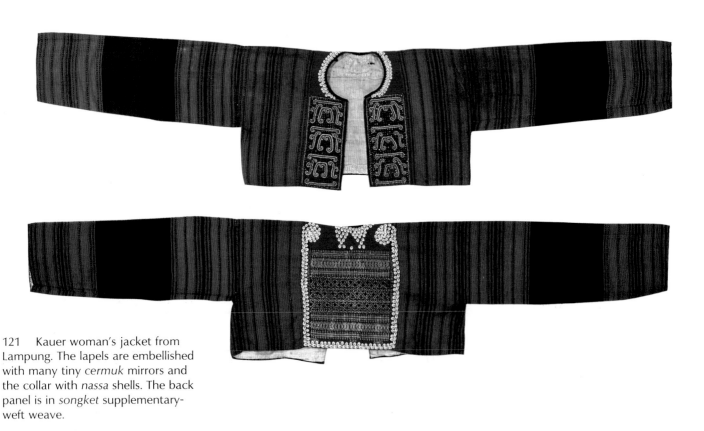

121   Kauer woman's jacket from Lampung. The lapels are embellished with many tiny *cermuk* mirrors and the collar with *nassa* shells. The back panel is in *songket* supplementary-weft weave.

122   Woman's cotton appliqué jacket made by the Kenyah Dyaks of Kalimantan.

123 (Right) The border of a woman's sarong from Ayotupas, west Timor. The motifs of lizards, birds and human figures are executed either in embroidery or by the *sungkit* technique.

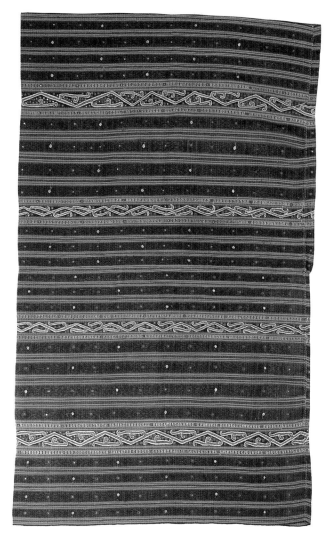

124 *Tapis* ceremonial skirtcloth of a Paminggir woman, adorned with figures of horses and riders in couched metal-thread embroidery, from coastal Lampung.

125 (Right) Kauer woman's *tapis* from Lampung, embroidered with bands of *cermuk* mirrors.

126 Detail of the *kepala* and *badan* of a silk *songket* sarong, from Singaraja, Bali.

127 Sarong from Karangasem, Bali, with floral motifs worked in the *songket* technique.

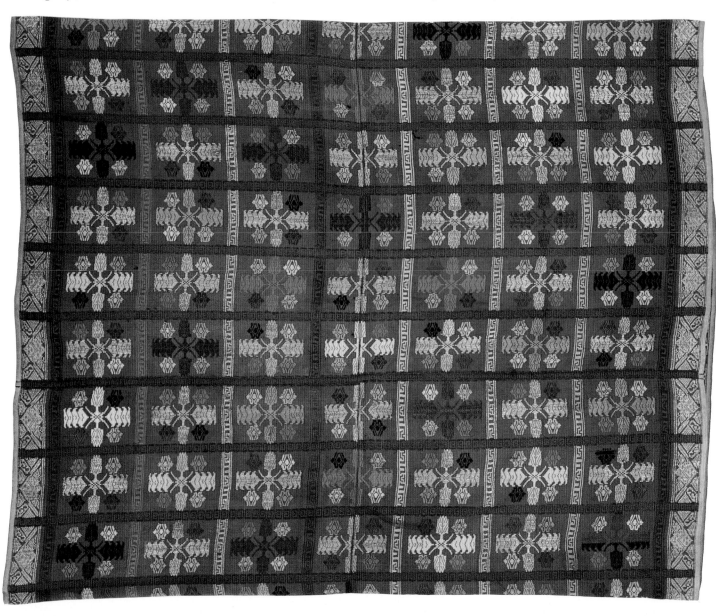

129 (Above) *Kamben songket* breastcloth from Karangasem, Bali, with floral motifs worked in silk supplementary weft on a silk ground.

128 (Left) Silk *songket* waistcloth from Singaraja, Bali.

130 (Left) *Tampan* cotton supplementary-weft ritual cloth, made by the people from the mountainous interior of Lampung.

131 (Above) Bark-cloth jacket from central Kalimantan.

132 Taman women in beadwork *bidang* skirts, and beadwork and shellwork jackets, from Putussibau, Upper Kapuas river, Kalimantan.

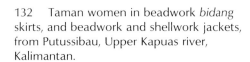

133 Beadwork baby sling, embellished with shell-money on an acrylic cloth border, made by the Kenyah Dyaks of Sarawak.

134 Supplementary-weft sarong from the Manggarai region of west Flores.

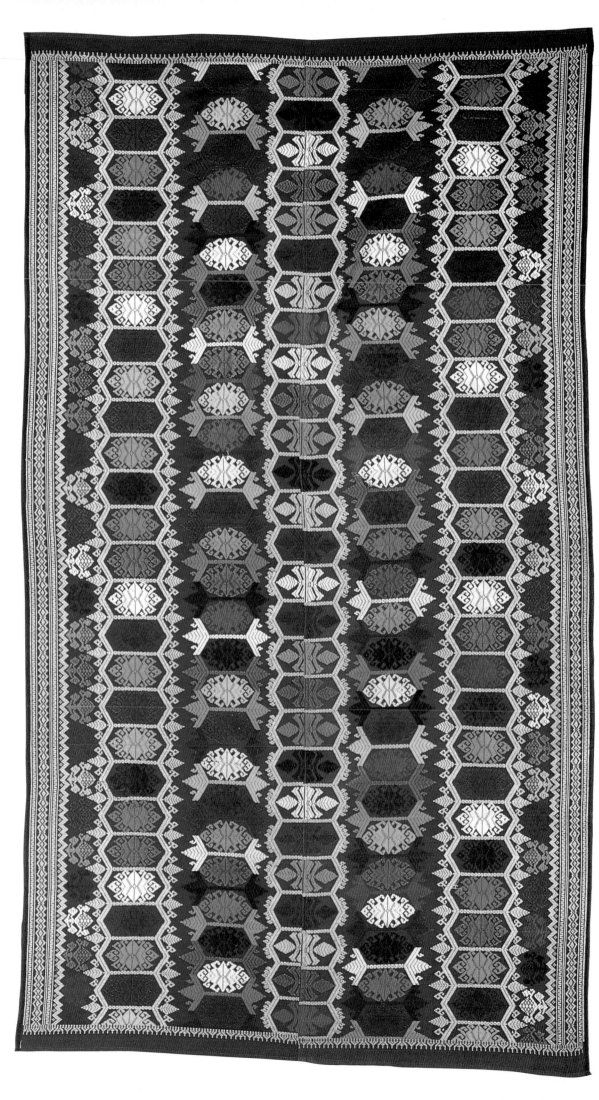

136 (Above) *Bidang* skirtcloth decorated in the *sungkit* warp-wrapping technique by the Iban Dyaks of Sarawak.

137 *Songket* sarong from Sumatra. The supplementary metal threads are worked into motifs of hibiscus flowers on the *badan* and cockerels' tails on the *kepala* decorative panel.

135 (Opposite) *Songket* waistcloth, artificial silk on a cotton ground. Jembrana, Bali.

138

139

141

140

138 Man's cotton sash, decorated with supplementary-warp motifs of leopards or civet cats, from east Sumba.

139 Supplementary-warp cotton sash with lizard motifs, from east Sumba.

140 Figures of cats worked in the supplementary-warp technique on a cotton sash from east Sumba.

141 Cotton sash from east Sumba with a twill pattern featuring female figures in the supplementary-warp technique.

142 Motifs of canopied women riding elephants adorn this extra-warp sash from east Sumba.

143 *Lurik* cotton cloth from Bali.

144 Cotton *lurik selendang* from Surakarta.

142

143

144

145 An aristocratic woman's *lau pahudu* skirt with a supplementary-warp border of human figures and animals, from east Sumba.

146   Supplementary-warp decorated sarong from Dili, east Timor.

147   (Opposite) Detail of the supplementary-warp border of a man's *selimut*, Ayotupas, west Timor.

148   *Ma'a* cotton
ritual cloth of the
Toraja of Sulawesi,
painted with a central
motif of sacrificial
buffalo being led into a
corral surrounded by
block-printed crosses
symbolizing stars.

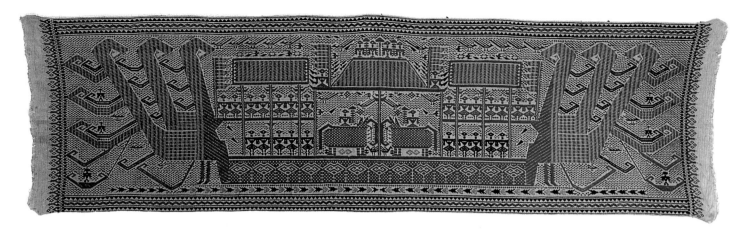

149 A *palepai* cotton textile used in the series of gift exchanges that take place at rites of passage in Lampung. Decorated in the supplementary-weft technique with the 'ship of the dead' motif.

150 The *ulos-ragidup* is ritually the most important of Batak textiles. Woven in three sections, the end panels are embellished with fine supplementary-weft patterning.

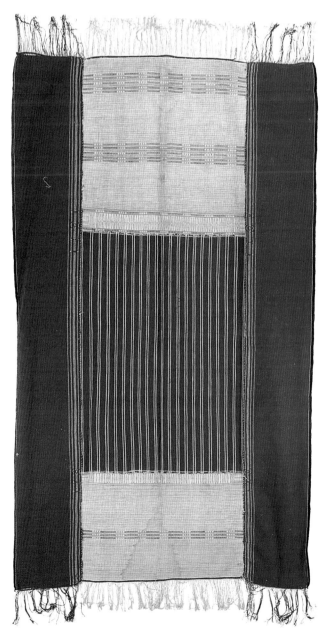

Sumatra is separated from neighbouring west Malaysia by the Straits of Malacca. Vast and relatively sparsely populated, it is the Indonesian island most richly endowed with natural resources. Having long-standing trading connections with India, China, Europe and Arabia, Sumatra is home to many distinct ethnic groups and boasts the most diverse textile tradition of the whole archipelago.

The Islamic Acehnese, the highland Batak, the matrilineal Minangkabau, the Malays of the eastern coast and the tribal groups of pepper-rich Lampung produce a wide variety of silk and cotton textiles in the techniques of warp and weft ikat, supplementary-weft weaving, metal-thread embroidery, plangi, tritik, and a distinctive style of batik.

Sumatra

Java

151 Batik *kain* with *cap*-printed motifs of storks from central Java.

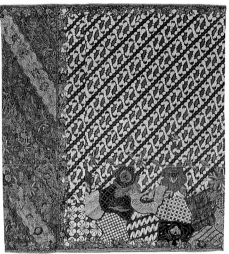

152 Detail of a *tiga negri* (three-country) *tulis*-batik sarong from north and central Java. The *badan* features the *garis miring* diagonally slanted design combined with *tambal* patchwork motifs.

153 (Opposite) Detail of a very fine *tiga negri* batik *kain* worked in *tulis* in north and central Java.

Java has both a Hindu and Buddhist past, and is proud possessor at Borobudur of the largest Buddhist monument in existence. It is now one of the most densely populated islands on earth, and the Javanese people are highly cultured, leavening the formalism of their Islamic beliefs with an admixture of native animism. Their art forms are particularly vibrant and the *wayang* puppet dramas draw heavily on the Indian legends of the *Mahabharata* and the *Ramayana*.

Although Java also manufactures weft-ikat, plangi, tritik, and *lurik* cloth, its block-printed and hand-drawn batik textiles are to be found everywhere. They are worn by market women and courtiers alike, transported in *becak* cycle-rickshaws and produced in startlingly bright colours in the large workshops of the north coast. They are also painstakingly worked in muted shades of indigo blue and *soga* brown in tiny workshops within the *kraton* courts of central Java. The main centres for batik production are Jogjakarta and Surakarta in central Java, and Cirebon and Pekalongan on the north coast.

Bali

154   Silk *songket* sarong from Karangasem.

155   *Endek* silk weft-ikat *selendang* with the 'Garuda's wings' design, a *banji*-derived central panel and *songket* borders, from Singaraja.

156   (Opposite) Detail of a *songket* temple hanging from Klungkung. Designs of *Dewi Sri*, the rice goddess, parasols, and flowers are worked in supplementary weft metal threads on a silk ground.

Bali, once an island paradise of legendary beauty, is now a major tourist resort. The Hindu-Buddhist Balinese are lovers of music, dance and religious festivals, which are celebrated with the ostentatious display of fine cloth. In villages that once acted as workshops to the local courts, fine *songket* metal-thread brocades, silk and cotton weft-ikat and plangi cloths are woven in all the colours of the rainbow. At Tenganan village, the Bali Aga are one of the few peoples of the world who can make double-ikat cloth. The double-ikat *kamben geringsing* woven there is revered and reserved for ritual use all over Bali.

Kalimantan, Sarawak, Sulawesi

157 (Right) Taman woman's jacket decorated with *nassa* shells, from the Upper Kapuas river, Kalimantan.

158 Front and rear view of a Taman woman's beadwork jacket, from the Upper Kapuas river, Kalimantan.

Kalimantan (Indonesian Borneo), rich in tropical rain forest, oil and minerals, is sparsely populated. The formerly head-hunting Dyaks live by the vast rivers of the interior jungles, and Malay peoples inhabit the coastal regions. The Dyaks produce textiles of beadwork, bark-fibre, or warp-ikat, and the coastal Malays weave fine *songket* brocade and embroider with metal thread. (157, 158)

Sarawak Now part of Malaysian Borneo, richly forested Sarawak was once ruled by the white rajas of the Brooke dynasty. It is inhabited by Chinese and Malays on the coast and Dyak groups in the interior. The Iban people, once the most aggressive head-hunters of all Borneo, form the main Dyak tribe. Iban women weave probably the most interesting textiles of the whole Indonesian-Malaysian area, working fantastical interlocking designs of magical significance on to *pua kumbu* ritual hangings and articles of clothing in the warp-ikat, *sungkit* and *pilih* techniques. (159, 160, 161)

Sulawesi Lying at the centre of the Indonesian archipelago, Sulawesi, with its four peninsulas, was at first mistaken by the Portuguese for a group of islands and named the Celebese. South Sulawesi is home to the fiercely independent, deeply Islamic Bugis and Makassarese. In their sailing *prahus*, these hardy seafarers penetrated the whole archipelago; their sometimes piratical trading activities reached as far as the north coast of Australia long before the advent of the Europeans. In the central highlands live the Christian and animist Toraja, famous for their intricately carved boat-shaped houses and for the great burial feasts that are celebrated with the ritual mass-slaughter of pig and buffalo. The Christian Minahasa Peninsula to the north was long an area of Dutch dominance. The main textile-producing regions are situated amongst the Bugis and the Toraja. The Bugis rear silkworms and weave *songket* cloth and cotton or silk weft ikat in iridescent colours. The Toraja create most striking textiles, including great funeral shrouds vividly patterned with geometric motifs in warp-ikat, and painted and block-printed cotton ritual cloths with naive depictions of tethered buffalo and cross-shaped stars. (162, 163, 164, 165)

159   Front and rear view of an Iban child's jacket worked with motifs of head-hunters and *engkaramba* spirit figures in the *pilih* floating extra-weft technique. Sarawak.

162   (Right) Tablet-woven belt of cotton, with motifs in Arabic script of magical significance. South Sulawesi.

161   (Below) Jacket of an Iban woman of Sarawak, decorated in the *sungkit* warp-wrapping technique.

160   *Sirat* loincloth decorated in the *sungkit* technique with embroidered details, made by the Iban people of Sarawak.

163   A Toraja man's satin trousers with *songket* cuffs. South Sulawesi.

164   (Opposite) Silk weft-ikat yardage from Sengkang.

165   Plaid-patterned silk sarong from the south.

Sulawesi

Lombok, Flores

Lombok Lying just to the east of Bali, Lombok is an island of contrasting climates and religions. The central plain is the main area of habitation, and lies between the mountainous north of the island and the barren arid south. The Hindu Balinese-dominated west is a land of lush rice fields, whilst the home of the indigenous Muslim and animist Sasaks to the east is drier and prone to famine. Cakranegara and Surakara are noted centres of textile manufacture, producing *songket* and weft-ikat cloth in patterns virtually indistinguishable from those of Bali. (166)

Flores On this long, lush, beautiful 'isle of flowers' are woven some of the world's most finely detailed warp-ikat textiles. The women of Lio and Sikka districts memorize figurative and *patola*-inspired motifs and tie them into cotton warp-yarns and then, after successive dyeings with indigo and *morinda citrifolia*, weave narrow widths of cloth on simple backstrap looms. Warp-ikat sarongs are produced for domestic use and for the commercial market in and around the coastal towns of Ende and Maumere and at the villages of Jopu, Wolonjita, and Nggela, near Mount Kelimutu. More simply patterned warp-ikat textiles are woven at Bajawa and around Larantuka, and in west Flores the Manggarai people wear indigo-dyed sarongs decorated with supplementary-weft work. (167, 168)

166   Ritual textile worked with borders of human figures in the supplementary weft technique by the Sasak people of Lombok.

167   Figurative warp-ikat cotton sarong from Nggela, Flores.

168 Extra-weft sarong of the Manggarai people, Flores, showing the tapestry-woven borders.

169   Ceremonial sash with a pattern of male figures and trees worked in cotton on a cotton ground in the supplementary-warp technique. East Sumba.

170   (Below) The obverse and reverse of a *hinggi* mantle with motifs of women and reptiles, worked in warp-ikat in the central field and in supplementary-warp on the borders. Pau, east Sumba.

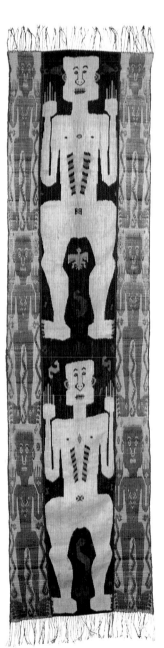

171   (Right) Ceremonial *lau pahudu* skirt with an extra-warp border of men and skull-trees, from east Sumba.

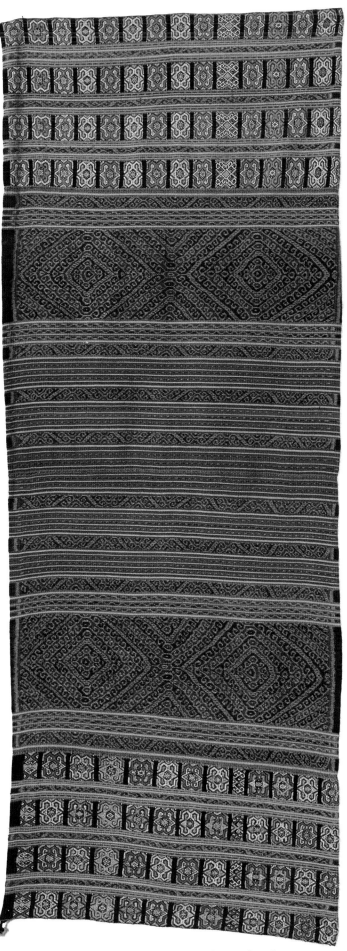

Sumba Once a great source of sandalwood, the island was divided into many mutually feuding petty principalities. It is the one island in the Indonesian archipelago where the majority of the population still hold to the indigenous animist beliefs. Every year the west Sumbans, so fond of their hardy horses and not averse to bloodshed, stage the *pasola* – a mock cavalry battle on the coastal plains. In dry east Sumba are woven the great cotton warp-ikat *hinggi* mantles that once served as shoulderwraps and hipcloths for royalty. The layout of the figurative mystical designs is most probably derived from ancient Chinese religious paintings. Warp-ikat *hinggis* are woven at Rende and Kaliuda and at Prailiu and Pau, which are also centres for supplementary warp-weaving. (169, 170, 171)

Timor is a long arid island which lies to the north of Australia. Kupang, the capital of both west Timor and the whole of east Nusa Tenggara, was long a centre of Dutch influence. Timor – particular the western half – has many centres for fine warp-ikat and supplementary-warp decorated textiles. Niki-Niki, Ayotupas, Kefa, Molo, Beboki, Maliana, Viveke and Los Palos have differing styles but common themes of anthropomorphic figures and bird and reptile life worked in bright colours. (172, 173)

172 (Above left) Warp-ikat *selendang* from Niki-Niki, west Timor.

173 (Above) Women's sarong from Ayotupas, west Timor. The borders are decorated in the *sungkit* technique and stripes of warp-ikat adorn the central field.

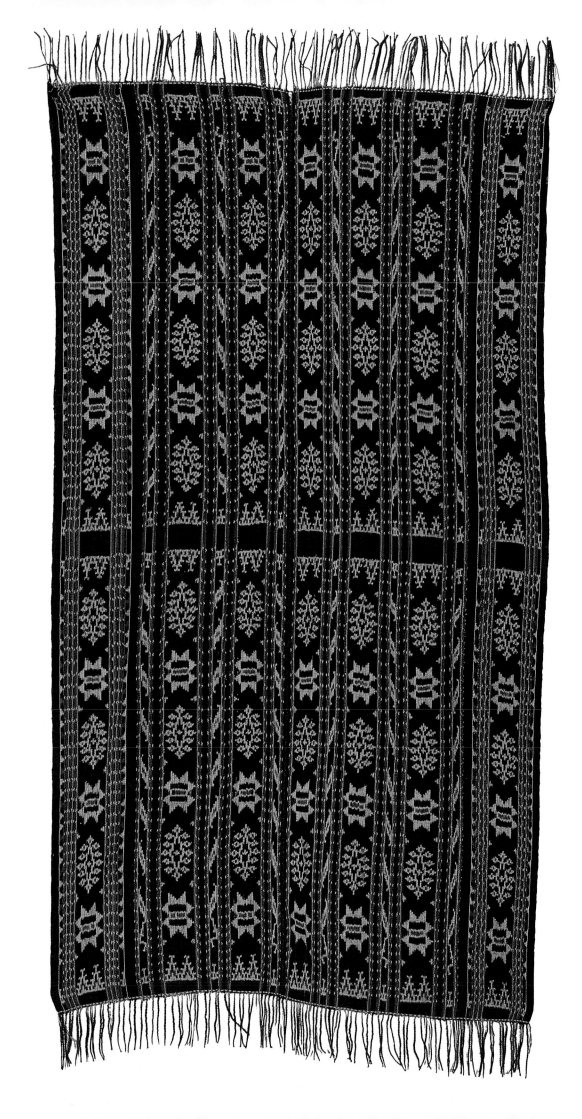

Savu, Rote

Savu and Rote are neighbouring islands that lie between Sumba and Timor. They are predominantly dry islands, whose peoples share Christian and animist beliefs. They produce palm wine and cotton sarongs and *selendangs* decorated in warp-ikat with European-influenced floral motifs.

174   (Opposite) Warp-ikat *selendang* of the 'Greater Blossom' clan of Savu.

175   Warp-ikat *selendang* with *patola*-influenced motifs from Rote.

176   *Wayang golek* puppets from central Java wearing batik sarongs.

Glossary

ABACA Fibre obtained from the leaves of the wild banana plant (*Musa textilis*).

ADAT Customary law that traditionally governs Indonesian social and religious life.

ALAS-ALASAN 'Virgin forest' batik design depicting flora and fauna, and symbolizing crop fertility.

ANILINE DYES Aniline is a chemical dyestuff derived from coal tar. The term can also be applied to all synthetic non-organic dyes.

A.T.B.M. '*Alat Tenun Bukan Mesin*' semi-mechanized fly-shuttle loom used all over Indonesia.

ATONI Tribal group from Timor.

BADAN Body of a sarong, usually about three-quarters of the length of the cloth.

BAHASA INDONESIA National *lingua franca* of Indonesia.

BALI AGA Inhabitants of Tenganan Pegeringsingan village, north-east Bali.

BANJI Chinese-derived word for 'swastika'. A common batik motif.

BARONG Iban protective spirit that inhabits the hornbill bird.

BAST Fibre obtained from the stem structure of dicotyledonous plants.

BATAK Tribal group from the highlands of northern Sumatra.

BELU Tribal group from Timor.

BIDANG Short tubular skirt worn by women of the Iban or other Dyak tribes of Borneo.

BUGIS Islamic seafaring ethnic group from south Sulawesi.

CAG-CAG Balinese body-tension loom.

CANTING Small wooden-handled instrument with a spouted copper reservoir, with which hand-drawn *tulis* batik is made.

CAP Copper stamp used to apply wax patterns in block-printed batik.

CEPLOKAN Category of geometric batik patterns based on repetitions of squares, rectangles, ovals and stars.

CEPUK Ritual weft-ikat cloth from Bali or neighbouring Nusa Penida.

CERMUK Small mirrored pieces of glass embroidered on to cloth in Sumatra.

CETAK Quick, commercial ikat dyeing process whereby different chemical dye-colours are spooned on to the required areas of the warp or weft threads, which are then bound with a resist and dip-dyed in the background colour.

CHINTZ Mordanted and dyed cotton textile from south-east India.

CINDE The name by which *patola* silk double-ikat cloth is known in Java and Sumatra.

COLETAN Quick commercial batik dye process whereby different-coloured chemical dyes are applied to required areas, waxed over and then dip-dyed in the background colour.

COMBINASI Batik cloth which is patterned using a combination of *canting* and *cap*.

COUCHED Embroidery technique in which decorative threads are tacked with small stitches to the surface of the cloth.

DANDONG Iban man's shoulder cloth.

DEWI SRI The rice goddess of Bali.

DODOT Large batik cloth worn by royalty, courtiers and dramatic artistes in central Java.

DONG-SON Name given to the Bronze-Age culture from northern Vietnam that had a very strong influence on culture and design in the Indonesian islands.

DOUBLE IKAT Ikat resist-dyeing process which is applied separately to both warp and weft threads. These are woven in a balanced plainweave so that the resulting fabric is patterned in designs that are a compound of the differently patterned warp and weft threads.

DUA NEGRI (lit. 'two country') Batik waxed and dyed in two different areas of Java.

ENDEK Weft-ikat cloth of silk or artificial fibre woven in Bali.

ENGKARAMBA Spirit figure of the Iban Dyaks of Sarawak.

FENG-HUAN The mythical Chinese phoenix bird, now a textile motif.

FUYA The term for bark cloth in Sulawesi.

GARIS MIRING Category of diagonally slanted batik designs from central Java.

GARUDA The winged mount of the Hindu god Vishnu.

GERINGSING Double-ikat cloth woven in the Balinese village Tenganan Pegeringsingan.

GIGI BARONG (lit. 'Barong's teeth') Pattern of white triangles along the borders of Balinese *cepuk* cloth.

GRINGSING Fish-scale pattern. One of the oldest motifs in Javanese batik.

HALUS Javanese term meaning 'fine'.

HEDDLE Essential part of a loom used to create the shed openings through which the weft threads are passed.

HINGGI Man's warp-ikat mantle from Sumba.

HOKUKAI Complex finely patterned batik made on the north Java coast during World War II, named after a Japanese political organization.

IBAN The dominant Dyak tribe of Sarawak, north Borneo.

IKAT The resist-dyeing process in which designs are reserved in warp or weft yarns by tying off small bundles of threads with fibre resists to prevent the penetration of dye.

INDISCHE Batik entrepreneurs of the north Javanese coast, of Eurasian or Dutch descent.

ISEN A category of batik background patterns.

JELAMPRANG Batik and ikat design found all over Indonesia, derived from the eight-petalled lotus *patola* motif.

JUMPUTAN Central Javanese term for plangi or tritik.

KAIN Cloth, generally rectangular, to be wrapped around the body. Often combined with a descriptive word – for example, *kain songket*, meaning cloth of *songket* weave.

KAIN LIMAR Cloth woven in Sumatra of weft-ikat silk with *patola*-derived patterning. Often combined with a *songket* border or field elements.

KAIN PANJANG 'Long cloth' worn as a waistcloth by both sexes.

KAIN SIMBUT Ritual cloth daubed with mystical signs in rice-paste batik from Banten in west Java.

KALLIGRAFI Style of batik based on quotations from the Koran, worked in Jambi or on the north Java coast for the Sumatran market.

KANDAURE Beadwork cover of the Toraja, south Sulawesi.

KAUER Ethnic group from Lampung, south-west Sumatra.

KAWUNG Category of batik patterns made up of groups of four ovals.

KEMBEN (Known as *kamben* in Bali) Breastcloth.

KEMIRI Candle-nut (*Aleurites mollucana*).

KEPALA The 'head' of the sarong. A broad perpendicular band of different colouring and patterning to that of the *badan*, or body, of the sarong.

KLOWONG The first waxing of a batik of such a consistency that it may be easily scraped off after the first dyeing.

KOMBU One common Indonesian term for the red dye derived from the root bast of *Morinda citrifolia* (see also *mengkudu*).

KRATON A Javanese palace.

LAMAK Long, narrow cotton or palm-leaf banner hung on tall poles or from temple entrances in Bali.

LAR One-winged Garuda motif in central Javanese batik.

LAU Woman's tubular skirtcloth from Sumba. *Lau hada* are decorated with shells and beadwork – *lau pahudu* with supplementary-warp borders.

LEMBA Wild grass (*Curculigo latifolia*). The fibres are used by the Iban of Sarawak to tie the resists for their warp-ikat, and are also used as yarn to weave warp-ikat cloth by the Benuaq of the Mahakam River area of east Kalimantan.

LOKCAN Batik of Chinese-inspired patterning, worked on Shantung silk in the Juana area of north Java.

LUKA SEMBA Warp-ikat *selendang*, patterned with *patola*-derived motifs worn by a clan leader in the Lio district of Flores.

MA'A Painted and block-printed cotton ritual textile of the Toraja, south Sulawesi.

MALOH Dyak tribe inhabiting the upper reaches of the Kapuas river, Borneo.

MANANG Shaman of the Iban Dyaks, Sarawak.

MAMULI Vulva-shaped metal ornament of great ritual significance that forms part of the bride price in Sumba.

MENGKUDU One Indonesian term for the red dye derived from the root bast of *Morinda citrifolia* (see also *kombu*).

MINANGKABAU Matrilineal ethnic group from western Sumatra.

MING Chinese imperial dynasty (1368–1644).

MORDANT Chemical that fixes a dye on fabric by combining with the dyestuff to form an insoluble compound.

MURUT Dyak tribe of Kalimantan.

NAGA Chinese-inspired dragon or snake motif.

NASSA Small cowrie-type shells (*Arcularia globosa* or *Arcularia thersites*).

NYATRI Balinese name for the *cetak* ikat-dyeing process.

PAGI-SORE 'Morning-evening' batik cloth, slightly longer than the *kain panjang*. Each half is of a different colour and design.

PARANG Diagonally slanted batik designs. Of the

many *parang* variants the *parang rusak* (broken knife) is the most famous and most revered.

PASOLA   Mock cavalry battle fought annually in west Sumba

PATOLA   Silk double-ikat textile from north-west India. Historically, widely traded and widely influential right across South-East Asia.

PATOLA RATU   Indonesian name for a *patola*-derived ikat pattern.

PALEPAI   1–3 yards-long supplementary-weft ritual cloth from Lampung, south-west Sumatra. Usually decorated with a 'ship of the dead' pattern.

PAMINGGIR   Ethnic group from Lampung, south-west Sumatra.

PAUF   One term by which supplementary-warp decoration is known in Timor.

PLANGI (or pelangi) (lit. 'rainbow').   Resist-dyeing process commonly known as tie-and-dye, whereby areas of cloth are bound off with dye-resistant fibres prior to dyeing. The resultant pattern is usually of small circles.

PILIH   Unique form of continuous supplementary-weft weaving practised by the Iban of Sumatra.

PORI LONJONG   Long warp-ikat textile woven by the Toraja of Sulawesi.

PRADA (or perada)   Decoration of cloth, by the glueing-on of gold leaf or gold dust.

PUA   Large warp ikat or *sungkit* ritual cloth of the Iban of Sarawak.

PUCUK REBUNG   Bamboo-shoot textile motif.

REED   A toothed piece of loom apparatus (also known as a comb), which acts as a warp-spacer and which is used to beat in the newly inserted weft-thread.

SAPPAN WOOD   The wood of *Caesalpinia sappan*, from which a red dye is obtained.

SASAK   The indigenous inhabitants of Lombok.

SARITA   Long cotton banners of indigenous rice-paste batik, or of Dutch industrial manufacture, employed for ritual use or for clothing by the Toraja

of Sulawesi.

SARONG   Tubular waistcloth.

SAWAT   Central Javanese batik motif of Garuda's wings and tail.

SEKO MANDI   Warp-ikat funeral shroud of the Toraja of Sulawesi.

SELENDANG   Shawl, usually a narrow rectangular cloth worn over the shoulder.

SELIMUT   Large shawl or mantle.

SEMEN   Category of figurative batik background patterns.

SIRAT   Iban man's loincloth.

SIRIH   Areca-nut and betel-leaf combined with lime and other ingredients. This is a widely taken stimulant in South-East Asia, which plays an important part in social rituals.

SOGA   A brown dye characteristic of central Javanese batik, derived from the bark of the *soga* tree (*Pelthophorum ferrugineum*).

SONGKET   Cloth patterned with the supplementary weft technique, where the supplementary wefts, usually of metal thread or silk, differ in material and texture from the ground weft threads.

SOTIS   A term for the supplementary warp technique used in Timor.

SUNGKIT   Decorative technique in which discontinuous supplementary wefts are worked on a passive warp between two regular wefts.

SUPPLEMENTARY WARP   (also known as extra-warp) A weaving technique in which an additional set of warp threads is woven into a textile to create a decorative pattern.

SUPPLEMENTARY WEFT   (also known as extra-weft) A weaving technique in which additional ornamental weft threads are woven into a textile between two regular wefts.

TABBY   (also plainweave) The simplest interlacing of warp and weft threads in a 'one-over, one-under' plainweave.

TAMAN   Branch of the Maloh Dyaks living on the upper Kapuas river, Kalimantan.

TAMBAL MIRING   'Patchwork' batik design.

TAMPAN   Square supplementary-weft ritual textile from Lampung, south-west Sumatra.

TAPESTRY WEAVE   Weft-faced plainweave, with discontinuous, usually differently coloured, wefts woven back and forth within their own patterning areas.

TAPIS   Woman's sarong from south Sumatra.

TATIBIN   One-yard-long narrow supplementary-weft ritual cloth from Lampung, south-west Sumatra.

TEMBOKKAN   (lit. 'wall') Thick, dark malleable batik wax intended to remain on the cloth throughout the first and subsequent dyeings.

TIGA NEGRI   (lit. 'three country') Batik waxed and dyed in three different areas of Java.

TORAJA   Bugis term for the non-Islamic groups living in the highlands of south Sulawesi.

TRITIK   Resist process in which designs are reserved by sewing and gathering the cloth before dyeing.

TULIS   Batik process in which the wax patterns are drawn out by hand, using a *canting*.

UDAN LIRIS   'Light rain' batik motif that combines a variety of designs contained within parallel diagonal lines.

ULOS   Batak generic term for cloth – for example, *ulos ragidup*, ritually the most important of Batak cloths.

WARP IKAT   The ikat-resist dyeing process is applied only to the warp threads, to pattern them prior to weaving.

WAYANG   Puppets that are used to enact the dramas of the *Ramayana* and *Mahabharata* in Java and Bali.

WEFT IKAT   The ikat resist-dyeing process applied only to the weft threads, to pattern them prior to weaving.

Further Reading

Ave, Joop and Judi Achjadi (eds.), *The Crafts of Indonesia*, Times Editions, Singapore, 1988.

Bolland, Rita, 'Weaving a Sumba Woman's Skirt', in Th. P. Gallenstein, L. Langewis, and Rita Bolland, *Lamak and Malat in Bali and a Sumba Loom*, Royal Tropical Institute, Amsterdam, 1956, pp. 49–56.

Bühler, Alfred, *Turkey Red Dyeing in South and South-East Asia*, CIBA Review 39, 1941.

—, *Patola Influences in South-East Asia*, Journal of Indian Textile History 4, 1959.

Bühler, Alfred, Urs Ramseyer and N. Ramseyer-Gygi, *Patola and Geringsing*, Museum für Völkerkunde, Basle, 1975.

Chin, Lucas, *Cultural Heritage of Sarawak*, Sarawak Museum, 1987.

Covarrubias, Miguel, *Island of Bali*, Alfred A. Knopf, New York, 1937, reprinted Oxford University Press, Singapore, 1987.

Crystal, Eric, 'Mountain Ikats and Coastal Silks: Traditional Textiles in South Sulawesi', in Joseph Fischer (ed.), *Threads of Tradition, Textiles of Indonesia and Sarawak*, exhibition catalogue, Lowie Museum of Anthropology and the University Art Museum, Berkeley, California, 1979, pp. 53–62.

Djoemena, Niam S., *Batik, Its Mystery and Meaning*, Penerbit Djambatan, Jakarta, 1986.

—, *Batik and Its Kind*, Penerbit Djambatan, Jakarta, 1990.

Dyrenforth, Noel, *The Technique of Batik*, Batsford, London, 1988.

Elliott, Inger McCabe, *Batik: Fabled Cloth of Java*, Clarkson and Potter, Inc., New York, 1984.

Emery, Irene, *The Primary Structure of Fabrics*, Textile Museum, Washington DC, 1966.

Fischer, Joseph (ed.), *Threads of Tradition, Textiles of Indonesia and Sarawak*, exhibition catalogue, Lowie Art Museum of Anthropology and the University Art Museum, Berkeley, California, 1979.

Forman, Bedřich, *Indonesian Batik and Ikat*, Hamlyn, London 1988.

Fraser-Lu, Sylvia, *Handwoven Textiles of South-East Asia*, Oxford University Press, 1988.

—, *Indonesian Batik, Processes, Patterns and Places*, Oxford University Press, Singapore, 1986.

Gittinger, Mattiebelle, *Splendid Symbols, Textiles and Tradition in Indonesia*, Textile Museum, Washington DC, 1979, reprinted with additional illustrations. Oxford University Press, Singapore, 1985 and 1989.

—, (ed.), *To Speak with Cloth*, UCLA Museum of Cultural History, Los Angeles, 1989.

Haddon, A. C. and L. E. Start, *Iban or Sea Dyak Fabrics and Their Patterns*, Cambridge University Press, Cambridge, 1936, reprinted 1982.

Hauser-Schäublin, Brigitta, Marie-Louise Nabholz-Kartaschoff and Urs Ramseyer, *Balinese Textiles*, British Museum Press, London 1991.

Hitchcock, Michael, *Indonesian Textiles*, British Museum Press, London 1991.

—, *Indonesian Textile Techniques*, Shire Publications, Aylesbury, England, 1985.

Holmgren, Robert J., and Anita E. Spertus, *Early Indonesian Textiles from Three Island Cultures – Sumba, Toraja, Lampung*, Metropolitan Museum of Art, New York, 1989.

Irwin, John, and Veronica Murphy, *Batiks*, Victoria and Albert Museum, large picture book No. 28, Her Majesty's Stationery Office, London, 1969.

Johnstone, Pauline, *Turkish Embroidery*, Victoria and Albert Museum, London, 1985.

Kahlenburg, Mary Hunt (ed.), *Textile Traditions of Indonesia*, exhibition catalogue, Los Angeles County Museum of Art, Los Angeles, 1977.

Kartiwa, Dra. Suwati, *Indonesian Ikats*, Penerbit Djambatan, Jakarta, 1987.

—, *Songket Weaving in Indonesia*, Penerbit Djambatan, Jakarta, 1986.

Kooijman, Simon, *Ornamental Bark-cloth in Indonesia*, Rijksmuseum voor Volkenkunde, Leiden, 1963.

Langewis, Laurens and Frits A. Wagner, *Decorative Art in Indonesian Textiles*, C. P. J. van der Peet, Amsterdam, 1964.

Larsen, Jack Lenor, with A. Bühler, and B. and G. Solyom, *The Dyer's Art: Ikat, Plangi, Tritik*, Reinhold, 1976.

Leigh, Barbara, *Hands of Time: The Crafts of Aceh*, Penerbit Djambatan, Jakarta, 1989.

Lubis, Mochtar, *Indonesia: Land Under the Rainbow*, Oxford University Press, Singapore, 1990.

Macmillan Arensberg, Susan, *Javanese Batiks*, Museum of Fine Arts, Boston, 1978.

Majlis, Brigitte Khan, *Indonesische Textilien, Wege zu Göttern und Ahnen*, Museum für Völkerkunde, Cologne, 1984.

Maxwell, Robyn, *Textiles of South-East Asia*, Oxford University Press, Australia, 1990.

Munan, Heidi, *Sarawak Crafts*, Oxford University Press, Singapore, 1989.

National Museum of Singapore, *Ancestral Ships: Fabric Impressions of Old Lampung Culture*, 1987.

Nawawi, Norwani Mohd, *Malaysian Songket*, Kuala Lumpur, 1989.

Newman, Thelma R., *Contemporary South-East Asian Arts and Crafts*, New York, 1976.

Newton, D. and J. P. Barbier (eds.), *Islands and Ancestors: Indigenous Styles of South-East Asia*, Prestel, Germany, 1988.

Nooy-Palm, Hetty, 'Dress and Adornment of the Sa'dan-Toradja (Celebes, Indonesia)', *Tropical Man*, Vol. 2, 1969, pp. 162–94.

Ong, Edric, *Pua: Iban Weavings of Sarawak*, exh. cat., Atelier Society, Sarawak, 1986.

Raffles, Thomas Stamford, *The History of Java*, Black Parbury and Allen, London, 1817, reprinted Oxford University Press, Kuala Lumpur, 1982.

Roth, H. Ling, *Studies in Primitive Looms*, Ruth Bean, Carlton, 1977.

Selvanayagam, Grace Inpam, *Songket: Malaysia's Woven Treasure*, Oxford University Press, Singapore, 1990.

Sibeth, Achim, *The Batak*, Thames and Hudson, London, 1991.

Solyom, Bronwen, and Garrett Solyom, *Textiles of the Indonesian Archipelago*, exhibition catalogue, University Press of Hawaii, Honolulu, 1973.

—, *Fabric Traditions of Indonesia*, exhibition catalogue, Museum of Art, Washington State University and Washington State University Press, Pullman, 1984.

Taylor, Paul Michael and Lorraine V. Aragon, *Beyond the Java Sea: Art of Indonesia's Outer Lands*, Abrams, New York, 1991.

Tillema, Hendrik Freerk, *A Journey Among the People of Borneo in Word and Picture*, Oxford University Press, Singapore, 1989.

Veldhuisen-Djajasoebrata, Alit, *Weavings of Power and Might: The Glory of Java*, Museum voor Volkenkunde, Rotterdam, 1988.

University of Hawaii Art Gallery, The Art of Asian Costume, 1989.

Wallace, Alfred Russel, *The Malay Archipelago*, 2 vols., 1869, reprinted Dover, New York, 1962.

Warming, Wanda, and Michael Gaworski, *The World of Indonesian Textiles*, Kodansha, Tokyo, 1981.

Yoshimoto, Shinobu, *Systematic Study of Indonesian Textiles*, 2 vols., Shiko-sha Publishing Co., Kyoto, 1978.

Museums and Galleries
with Collections of Indonesian Textiles

The museums and galleries listed below have interesting collections of Indonesian textiles, either on display or in store; however, it is advisable to contact museums in advance to determine what textiles are on display. Most textile curators will grant access to their stored collections if an appointment is made.

AUSTRALIA
Canberra Australia National Gallery, Lake Burley Griffin, Canberra City, A.C.T.; **Darwin** Museums and Art Galleries of the Northern Territory, P.O. Box 4646, Darwin, N.T.; **Sydney** Australian Museum, 6–8 College Street, Sydney, 2000 N.S.W.; **Townsville** Townsville University Museum, James Cook University, Townsville, Queensland

AUSTRIA
Vienna Museum für Völkerkunde, Neue Hofburg, A–1014 Vienna

BELGIUM
Brussels Musées Royaux d'Art et d'Histoire, 10 Parc du Cinquantenaire

BRUNEI
Begawan Brunei Museum, Kota Batu, Banda Seri, Begawan

CANADA
Ottawa National Museum of Man, Metcalfe/McLeod Sts, Ottawa, Ontario, KIA OM8; **Toronto** Royal Ontario Museum, 100 Queens Park, Toronto, Ontario M5S 2C6

CZECHOSLOVAKIA
Prague Naprstek Museum, Betlémské Námĕsti 1, Stare Mĕsto 11000, Prague 1

DENMARK
Copenhagen National Museum of Denmark, Ny Vestergade 10, Copenhagen

FRANCE
Lyons Musée Historique des Tissus, 34 rue de Charité, 69001 Lyon; **Mulhouse** Musée de l'Impression sur Etoffes, 3 rue des Bonnes-Gens, 68100 Mulhouse; **Paris** Musée Guimet, 6 Place d'Iéna, 75116 Paris: Musée de l'Homme, Palais de Chaillot, 75116 Paris

GERMANY
Berlin Museum für Indische Kunst, Takustrasse 40, 1000 Berlin; Museum für Völkerkunde, Arnimallee 23–27, 1000 Berlin; Pergamon Museum für Völkerkunde, Bode Strasse 1–3, 102 Berlin; **Cologne** Rautenstrauch-Joest-Museum, Ubierring 45, 5000 Köln, Nordrhein-Westfalen; **Frankfurt** Museum für Völkerkunde, Schaumainkai 29, 6000 Frankfurt; **Krefeld** Deutsches Textilmuseum Krefeld, Andreas Markt 8, 4150 Krefeld, Nordrhein-Westfalen; **Stuttgart** Linden-Museum, Hegelplatz, Stuttgart

HUNGARY
Budapest Neprajzi (Ethnographical) Museum, Kossuth Lajos ter 12, 1055 Budapest

INDONESIA
Bali
Denpasar Bali Museum (Museum Bali), Jl. Letnan Kolonel Wisjnu 8, Denpasar
Java
Bandung West Java Museum (Museum Negeri Jawa Barat), Jl. Oto Iskandar Dinata, Bandung; **Jakarta** Central Museum (Museum Pusat Lembaga Kebudajaan), Medan Merdeka Barat 12, Dil. Merdeka Barat, Jakarta; Indonesia Museum, Jl.

Taman mini Indonesia Indah, Bogor-Jakarta Highway, Jakarta; Textile Museum (Museum Textil), Jl. K. Satsuit Tuban 4, Jakarta; **Jepara** Museum Kartini Jepara, Jl. Kartini 1, Jepara; **Jogjakarta** Batik Museum, Jl. Dro Sutomo 96, Jogjakarta; Hamengku Buwono Palace Museum (Museum Hamengku Buwono), Jogjakarta; Memorial Museum (Dewantara Kirti Griya), Jl. Taman Siswa 31, Jogjakarta; Museum Angkatan Darat, Jl. Bintara Wetan 3, Jogjakarta; **Pekalongan** Batik Museum, Jl. Passar Ratu 30, Pekalongan; **Surabaya** Empu Tantular Museum (Museum Negeri Jawa Timur Mpu Tantular), Jl. Taman Mayangkara 6, Surabaya; Museum Tni A. L. Loka Jala Crana, Jl. Komp. Akabri Laut, Morokrambangan, Surabaya; **Surakarta** Museum Binatang Sriwedari, Jl. Slamet Riyadi 235, Surakarta; Museum Pers, Jl. Gajah Mada 59, Surakarta; Prince Mangkunegara Palace Museum (Museum Pura Mangkunegaran), Surakarta
Kalimantan
Pontianak Museum Negeri, Kalimantan Barat, Jl. Jend A. Yani, Pontianak
Riau
Tajung Pinang Kandil Riau Museum (Museum Swasta Kandil Riau), 76 Kp Melati Jalan Batu II, Tajung Pinang
Sulawesi
Ujung Pandang Lagaligo Museum, Ujung Pandang
Sumatra
Banda Aceh Aceh Museum (Museum Negeri Propinsi D.I. Aceh), Jl. Yapakeh 12, Banda Aceh; **Bukittinggi** Museum Bundo Kandung, Jl. Taman Puti Bungsu, Bukittinggi; **Medan** Museum Perjuangan Bukit Barisan, Jl. H. Zainal Arifin 8, Medan; North Sumatra Museum (Museum Negeri Sumatera Utara), Jl. H. Joni, Medan; **Padang** West Sumatra Museum (Museum Negeri Sumbar Aditya Arman), Jl. Kiponegoro (Lap. Tugu), Padang; **Palembang** Municipal Museum, Palembang; **Pematangsiantar** Museum Simalungun 20, Pematangsiantar

ITALY
Milan Museum of Far Eastern Art and Ethnography, Via Mose Bianchi, 94, Milan; **Rome** Luigi Pigorini Museum of Ethnography and Prehistory, Viale Lincoln 1, Rome

JAPAN
Osaka National Museum of Ethnology (Kokuritsu Minzokugaku Hakubutsukan) 23–17 Yamadaogawa, Suita-Shi, Osaka; Museum of Textiles, 5–102 Tomobuchi-Cho, 1-Chome, Miyakojima-Ku, Osaka

MALAYSIA
Malaya
Kuala Lumpur Museum of Asian Art, University of Malaya, Kuala Lumpur; National Art Gallery, 109, Ampang Road, Kuala Lumpur; National Museum Jl. Damansara, Kuala Lumpur
Sabah
Kota Sabah State Museum, 1239 Gaya St., Kota, Kinabalu
Sarawak
Kuching Sarawak Museum, Jl. Tun Haji Openg, Kuching

NETHERLANDS
Amsterdam Museum of the Royal Tropical Institute, Linnaeusstraat 2, 109AD Amsterdam; **Delft** Nusan Tara Ethnographical Museum, Agatha Plein 4, 2611

HR Delft; **Leiden** National Museum of Ethnography, Steenstraat 1, 2300 A.E. Leiden; **Rotterdam** Museum of Geography and Ethnology, Willemskade 25A, 3016 D.M. Rotterdam

PHILIPPINES
Manila National Museum of the Philippines, Manila

POLAND
Warsaw Asia and Pacific Museum (Muzeum Asji I Pacyfiku), Galeria Nusantary of Nowogrodska 18a, Warsaw

PORTUGAL
Lisbon Museum of Overseas Ethnography, Lisboa, Rua das Portas de Santo Antao, Lisbon

RUSSIA
Moscow Museum of Oriental Art, Ul. Obucha. 16. Moscow; **St Petersburg** Hermitage Museum, Nab. Dvortsovaja 36, St Petersburg; Peter the Great Museum of Anthropology and Ethnography, 3 Universitetshaya Naberezhnaya, St Petersburg

SINGAPORE
National Museum, Singapore 0617

SPAIN
Barcelona Museum of Ethnography, Parque de Montjuich, Barcelona; **Madrid** National Museum of Anthropology and Ethnology, Calle Alfonso XII 68, Madrid

SWEDEN
Gothenburg Ethnographical Museum, Norra Hamngatan 12, 41114 Gothenburg; **Stockholm** Ethnographical Museum, Djurgardsbrunnsvagen 34, 11527 Stockholm

SWITZERLAND
Basle Museum für Völkerkunde Augustinergasse 2, 4001 Basle; **St Gallen** Völkerkundliche Sammlung, Museumstrasse 50, 9000 St Gallen; **Zurich** Völkerkunde Museum der Universität, Pelikanstrasse 40, 8001 Zurich

UNITED KINGDOM
Bradford Cartwright Hall, Lister Park, Manningham, Bradford; **Bristol** Bristol City Museum, Queen's Road, Bristol BS8 1RL; **Cambridge** University Museum of Archaeology and Ethnology, Downing St, Cambridge; **Durham** Gulbenkian Museum of Oriental Art, University of Durham, Elvet Hill, Durham DH1 3TH; **Edinburgh** Royal Scottish Museum, Chambers Street, Edinburgh EH1 1JF; **Halifax** Bankfield Museum, Akroyd Park, Halifax HX3 6H6; **Leicester** Leicestershire Museum and Art Gallery, New Walk, Leicester; **London** British Museum, Department of Oriental Antiquities, Great Russell Street, London WC18 3DG; Embroiderers Guild, Apartment 41a, Hampton Court Palace, East Molesey, Surrey; Horniman Museum, Forest Hill, London SE23 8PQ; Museum of Mankind, 6 Burlington Gardens, London W1X 2EX; Victoria and Albert Museum, Cromwell Road, South Kensington, London SW7 2RL; **Manchester** The Whitworth Art Gallery, University of Manchester, Manchester M15 6ER; **Nottingham** Museum of Costume and Textiles, 51 Castle Gate, Nottingham NG1 6AT; **Oxford** Ashmolean Museum, Beaumont Street, Oxford OX1 2PH; Pitt-Rivers Museum, South Parks Road, Oxford OX1 3PP

UNITED STATES
Berkeley Lowie Museum of Anthropology, Kroebber Hall, Bancroft Way, University of California,

Berkeley, CA; **Boston** Museum of Fine Arts, 465 Huntington Ave, Boston MA; S.P.N.E.A., Harrison Gray Otis House, 141 Cambridge St, Boston, MA; **Cambridge** Peabody Museum of Archeology and Ethnology, Harvard University, 11 Divinity Ave, Cambridge, MA; **Chicago** Art Institute of Chicago, Michigan Ave at Adams St., Chicago, IL; Field Museum of Natural History, Roosevelt Rd at Lakeshore Drive, Chicago, IL; **Cincinnati** Cincinnati Museum of Fine Art, Eden Park, Cincinnati, OH; **Cleveland** Cleveland Museum of Art, 11150 East Boulevard, Cleveland, OH; **Denver** Denver Art Museum, 100 West 14th Ave, Parkway, Denver, CO; **Detroit** Detroit Institute of Arts, 5200 Woodward Ave, Detroit, MI; **Indianapolis** The Indianapolis Museum of Art, 1200 West 38 St, Indianapolis, IN; **Los Angeles** Los Angeles County Museum of Art, 5905 Wilshire Boulevard, Los Angeles, CA; Mingei International Museum of Folk Art, 4405 La Jolla, Village Drive, La Jolla. CA; Museum of Cultural History, University of California, 405 Hilgard Ave, Los Angeles, CA; **Newark** Newark Museum, 43–49 Washington Street, Newark, NJ; **New York City** American Museum of Natural History, 79th Street & Central Park West, New York City, NY; Brooklyn Museum, 188 Eastern Parkway, Brooklyn, New York City, NY; Cooper Hewitt Museum of Design, Smithsonian Institution, 5th Ave at 91st St., New York City, N.Y.; Metropolitan Museum of Art, 5th Ave at 82nd St, New York City, N.Y.; **Philadelphia** Philadelphia Museum of Art, Parkway at 26th St, Philadelphia, PA; **Salem** Peabody Museum of Salem, East India Square, Salem, MS; **San Francisco** M.H. de Young Memorial Museum, Golden Gate Park, San Francisco, CA; **Seattle** Historic Costume and Textile Collections, University of Washington, Seattle, WA; National Museum of Natural History, Seattle Art Museum, Volunteer Park, Seattle, WA; **Washington** National Museum of Natural History, Smithsonian Institution, Washington, DC; Textile Museum, 2320 S Street NW, Washington, DC.

Acknowledgments

Our thanks to: Suardi Adjas; Elizabeth Andrews; Nicholas Barnard; Richard Brigenshaw; Jane Brooks; Mary Geddes; Joel and Seth Gillow; Janet Harvey; Rudi Laurens; James Merrell; Photomail (Bradford); Rose Rands; School of Art and Design, Bradford and Ikley Community College; Alan Smith; Christine Sterne; Marianne Straub; Nelson Tan; Warrens Photolabs (Leeds); The Winston Churchill Trust; and Alex Wood, for all their help. We would especially like to thank Stephan Schorr-Kon for the loan of his extensive batik collection; Alan Jacobs and Lesley Parry for their collection of warp ikat; Paul Garrod and Rosalind Price of Chandni Chowk for their widely varied textile collection, and Diane and Jim Gaffney for the loan of batik-making implements and textiles; and lastly Alastair Hull both for the loan of his textile collection and for the unfailing generosity with which he availed us of his photographic facilities. I'd also like to acknowledge the works of S. Fraser-Lu, Mattiebelle Gittinger, Wanda Warming and Michael Gaworski, and Robyn Maxwell, to whose scholarship I am much indebted.

Illustration Acknowledgments

All colour photographs are by Barry Dawson, with the exception of the following: 80, 158 Paul Garrod; 132 John Gillow; 168 James Merrell. Black and white photographs on pages 8, 11, 12, 31, 43, 44, 46, 79 and 114 are reproduced by kind permission of VIDOC, Department of the Royal Tropical Institute, Amsterdam.

All line drawings are by Bryan Sentance, with the exception of those on pages 2–3, 6, 27, 48, 74, 82, 83, 87 and 88, which are by Eva Hehemann.

Index

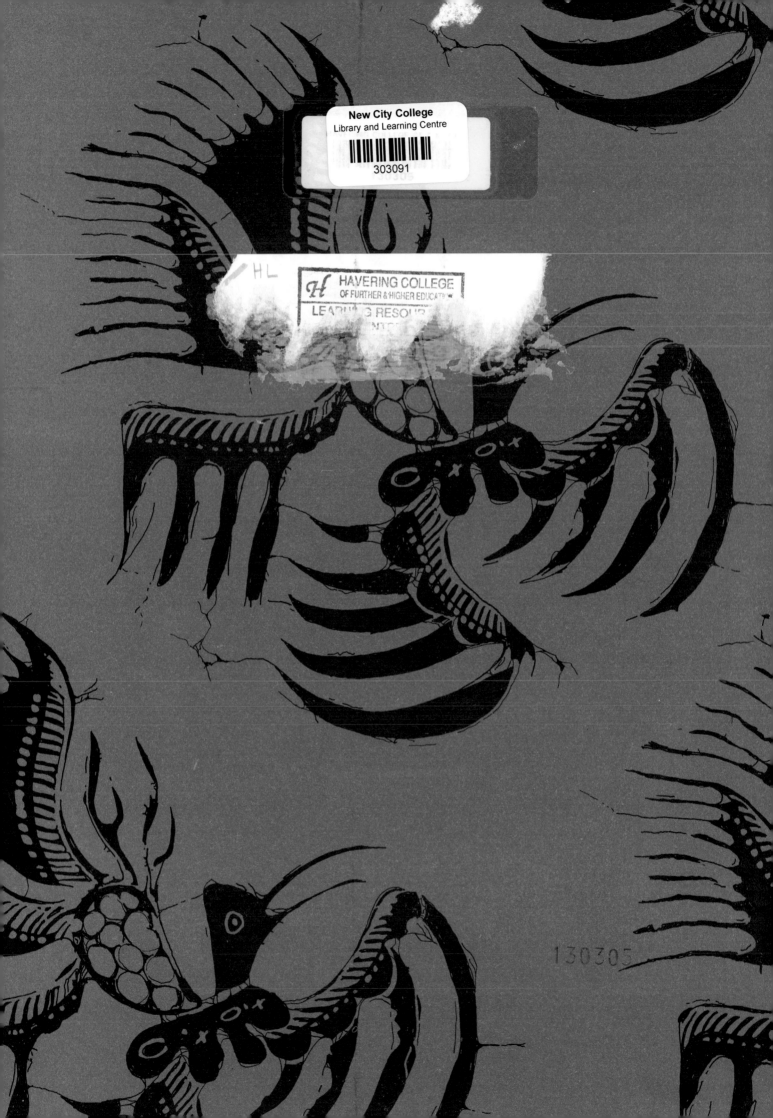